COASTAL WALKS

Llŷn Peninsula Coastal Walks

A DETAILED GUIDE TO A WALK AROUND THE COAST OF LLŶN

Richard A.R. Quine

ISBN: 0-86381-486-7

Cover photo: Aled Gruffydd

Cover design: Alan Jones

First published in 1999 by
Gwasg Carreg Gwalch, 12 Iard yr Orsaf, Llanrwst, Wales LL26 0EH
01492 642031 01492 641502
books@carreg-gwalch.co.uk   Web site: www.carreg-gwalch.co.uk

CONTENTS

Preface

Centuries ago people flocked in their thousands to this remote peninsula; pilgrims on their way to Ynys Enlli *(Bardsey Island)* three visits to which were considered the equal of one to Rome, and where 20,000 saints are reputed to be buried.

Today they come, tourists now, for many different reasons; sailors and swimmers and sand castle builders; fishermen and golfers; historians, archaeologists and geologists; botanists and ornithologists.

This book is dedicated to those who simply enjoy a good walk in idyllic surroundings with perhaps a passing interest in some of these activities.

Introduction

The Llŷn Peninsula is that finger of land in northern Wales that points south west into the Irish Sea, towards Ireland; it is bound on the north by Bae Caernarfon, on the south by Bae Ceredigion (*Cardigan Bay*) and to the east by the foothills of Snowdonia. It is roughly 25 miles long by an average of 8 miles wide, and has a coastline, from Caernarfon in the north to Porthmadog in the south, of approximately 95 miles, of which 55 miles have been designated an Area of Outstanding Natural Beauty and Heritage Coast. The National Trust owns some 12 miles and there are several Sites of Special Scientific Interest. The weather can be wet and windy but the climate is mild. There are wide sandy beaches, secluded coves, magnificent cliff scenery, open heathland, and towns and villages of character.

Apart from the enjoyment of wide open spaces and the sheer beauty of the area, there is something of interest for everyone. For the naturalist, there is a profusion of wild flowers and birds; for the geologist, some of the world's oldest rocks; for the archaeologist the remains of ancient civilisations; for the historically minded, there are fortifications from the Iron Age to W.W.11 and reminders of the areas industrial past; for the railway enthusiast there are narrow gauge lines. For much of the way we will be following in the footsteps of pilgrims, staying where they stayed, refreshing at their wells.

Cut off as the peninsula is by sea and mountains it is not surprising that the area became, and remains to this day, a stronghold of Welsh culture. Welsh is the first language of the locals, though all are nowadays bilingual, and signs are more often than not in both languages. As in any country it is considered polite and much appreciated if a few words can be spoken in the native tongue. Half a dozen spring to mind:

Croeso	Welcome
Bore da	Good morning
Nos da	Good night

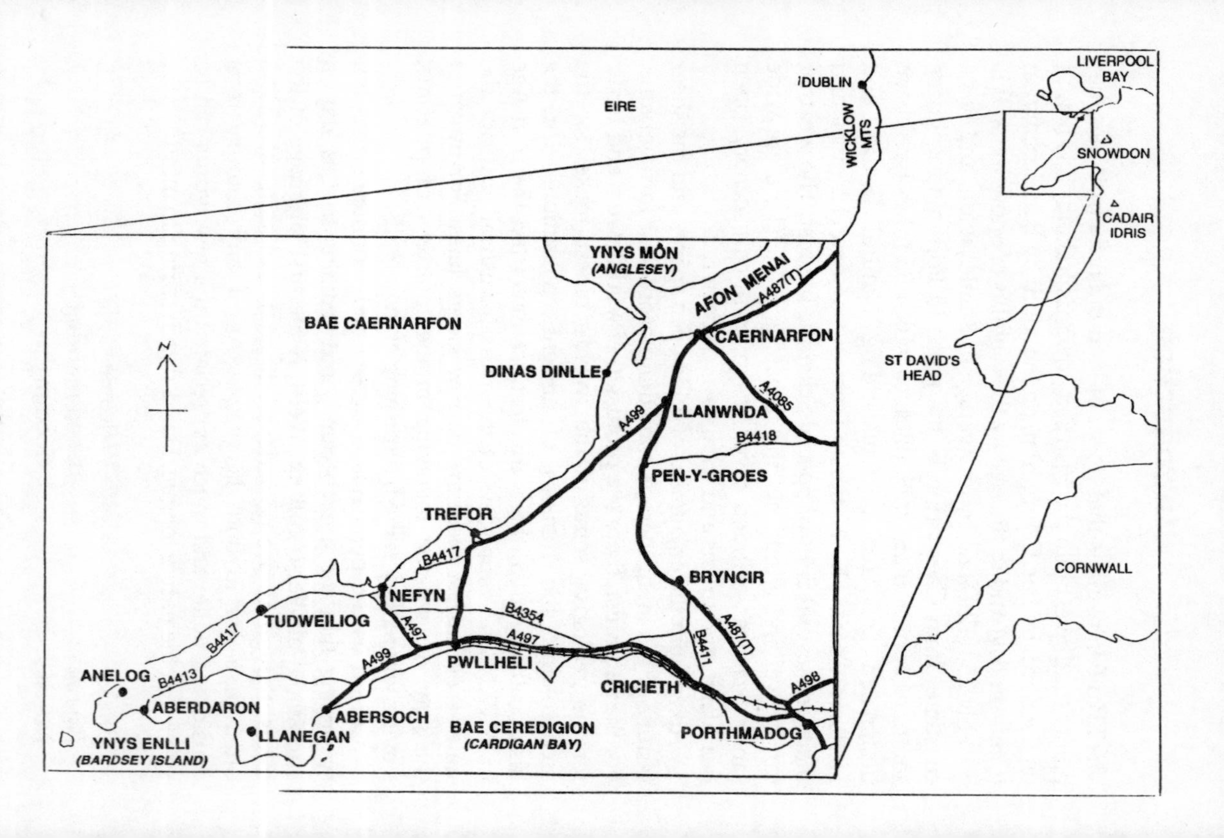

LIVERPOOL BAY
DUBLIN
EIRE
WICKLOW MTS
SNOWDON
CADAIR IDRIS
YNYS MÔN (ANGLESEY)
AFON MENAI
A487(T)
BAE CAERNARFON
CAERNARFON
DINAS DINLLE
ST DAVID'S HEAD
N
LLANWNDA
A499
A4085
B4418
PEN-Y-GROES
TREFOR
B4417
CORNWALL
NEFYN
BRYNCIR
TUDWEILIOG
B4354
A497
A497
B4411
A487(T)
B4417
A499
PWLLHELI
ANELOG
B4413
CRICIETH
A498
ABERDARON
ABERSOCH
BAE CEREDIGION (CARDIGAN BAY)
PORTHMADOG
YNYS ENLLI (BARDSEY ISLAND)
LLANEGAN

Diolch yn fawr	Thank you
Iechyd da	Good health

And to avoid possible embarrassment!

Dynion	Men
Merched	Women

Throughout we will use Welsh place names, with the English name where necessary in brackets. A glossary of the more common words that are likely to be encountered is given at the back.

This remoteness has produced two other results. Firstly a dependence on the sea, which in the old days provided the best means of contact with the larger world, produced a race of seafarers renowned in maritime circles, and this in turn spawned a shipbuilding industry as we shall see later. Secondly, it has left the area largely unspoilt by progress, and relatively under populated.

This then is the background to our walk. There is not as yet a clearly designated footpath around the coast, such as one finds on other long distance walks, and we therefore have to make use of local paths, beaches and even minor roads for short distances; but the way ahead is invariably obvious since we shall be following as close to the sea as possible. This lends more of a feeling of adventure to the walk, finding ones own way rather than just following a well trodden route. For this reason, and because paths and stiles have a habit of disappearing, a map is essential, (and even a compass might be useful). The Ordnance Survey Explorer 1:25 000 maps, no's 12 and 13, cover the whole route (except for a couple of miles at the start) and the O.S. Snowdonia National Park is a useful addition since it covers most of the area in sight, thus enabling distant landmarks to be identified.

The route can be described as easy to moderate with most of the way being at, or just above, sea level. Only at one point is there a fairly stiff climb to just over 1,100ft. A word of caution, particularly on the north coast, because a convex grass slope can often hide a sheer drop to the rocks below. Even dry grass can be very slippery, so that a watchful eye should be kept on children and dogs. Coastal erosion in some places has caused the cliffs to be undercut leaving an unstable edge and sometimes destroying the path altogether. Footwear is a matter of choice, but paths can get muddy and boggy in places. Sheep, of which there are more than humans in Wales, can very soon turn a dryish path into a river of mud, and stout waterproof boots are essential, but a good pair of trainers would be an useful addition for the beach and some of the drier places. As with any coastal path it can get very wet and windy so appropriate wind and water proof clothing is necessary.

A long distance walk should not be turned into a route march, and time should be taken to appreciate ones surroundings. Two miles an hour is about average with a daily distance of say twelve miles for the more inexperienced, though others may manage more. This criterion presents problems since, as previously mentioned, the area is sparsely populated and accommodation not always easy to find. Those who are camping will not have a problem since there are plentiful official and unofficial sites. For those who rely on finding a proper bed for the night, we have divided the book into chapters that take this into account. Some daily distances will therefore be longer and others shorter, than the ideal. It must be emphasised that accommodation should be booked in advance. Tourist offices in Caernarfon, Pwllheli and Porthmadog can help.

The route we have chosen does not necessarily imply a public right of way, but as far as possible we have followed official footpaths, and only strayed where we found it to be acceptable, such as on open moorland, headlands and beaches. The usual country code applies, particularly as far as gates, fences and dogs are concerned. On the subject of dogs, recent by-laws have banned them from certain popular beaches during the main tourist season i.e. 1st May to 30th September. This presents no problems for dog owners and we shall point out these beaches, and how to avoid them, as and when they arise. It is ideal walking for dogs and it would be a pity to deny them. At other times of the year there are no restrictions, other than the usual one of cleaning up after them.

Whether one walks from Caernarfon to Porthmadog or vice versa is a matter of personal choice but the former is, in the writer's opinion, preferable since in the second half of the walk one is walking towards the magnificent backdrop of Snowdonia and the views across Bae Ceredigion (*Cardigan Bay*). The complete walk of approximately 105 miles can be accomplished in a fortnight but for those who have neither the time nor the energy, it can be shortened by starting at Trefor and finishing at Pwllheli, which at 65 miles can be accomplished in a week.

Caernarfon can be reached by main line train to Bangor and then bus, whilst Porthmadog is on the Mid-Wales Cambrian Coast line. Both towns are connected to the National bus network.

It is appreciated that some people prefer to have the convenience of their own transport. With this in mind we give, at the end of each chapter, circular walks incorporating some of the finest sections of the coast covered by that particular chapter. These we have divided into two walks of approximately four miles each so that one can be taken in the morning and, after a short car ride, the other can be done in the afternoon, thus avoiding the necessity of carrying a heavy rucksack. The walks are a blend of coast and country, since the return journey to the car will inevitably be by an inland route. The peninsula is crisscrossed with footpaths and winding lanes that are largely devoid of people and vehicles, and which merit further exploration in their own right, but it is in the coastline that the true splendour lies.

These shorter walks should be read in conjunction with the main text. Taken together, the walks are aimed at the more serious walker for whom eight miles a day is acceptable, but they can be taken individually by the less energetic for a leisurely half day excursion. Times given are based on a steady walking pace, with no allowance for stops. Regrettably none of the walks are suitable for the disabled. To avoid needless repetition, the point at which the car walks join the route given in the main text is signified by (A) for walk 1 and (X) for walk 2, and where they leave the main route by (B) and (Y) respectively. The walks are graded as follows:-

Easy:	Level walk on roads or well maintained paths.
Moderate:	Some short sharp ups and downs, and paths not always well maintained.
Rough:	As moderate, but rough underfoot with overgrown paths and stiles.
Strenuous:	Long climbs, and rough underfoot.

Wales is famed for its fine beaches and the Llŷn peninsula is no exception. For those readers who may not be familiar with them, we list nineteen of the finest, giving a general description and details of parking, facilities etc. Note; facilities are unlikely to be open out of season. The beaches are also numbered in the main text.

Finally, for those who would like to make a quick recce. of the area, we give a whistle stop circular tour of the peninsula by car. Although we start in Caernarfon and proceed in an anti-clockwise direction, being circular, the route can be joined at any point.

It is hoped that this introduction has whetted your appetite for this truly magnificent peninsula, in which case, we say:

'Croeso i Ben Llŷn'.

A note on pronouncing Welsh place-names

If you're a visitor to Wales or you've recently come to live here, and you need to ask the way to somewhere, it can be a bit of a challenge. It's fine if you want to go to a place with a straightforward short name like Bangor or Corwen, but if you're heading for Rhosllannerchrugog, Llwyngwril or Llanrhaeadr-ym-Mochnant, you may be tempted to admit defeat and just point at the mind-bending string of letters in the guidebook.

If would be very satisfying, wouldn't it, to be able to reel off Troedrhiwdalar or Pontrhydfendigaid as easily as Birmingham or Newcastle? But most people are put off from even trying because they get the impression that the pronunciation of names like these must be very difficult, or even impossible, if you're not Welsh. They look at Betws-y-coed, for example, and can't work out what to do with the 'w', so they just leave it out and end up, as often as not, with that well-known Welsh schoolgirl, Betsy Co-Ed. Some of the Welsh used to believe they had longer tongues than the English, so they could pronounce words that the English couldn't, and when you're faced with something like Eglwyswrw or Llanuwchllyn, you could be forgiven for thinking they might have been right.

So let's get one thing clear straight away. The idea that Welsh pronunciation is difficult is *complete nonsense.*

Admittedly, if you wanted to acquire a perfect Welsh accent, you'd have to be prepared for a bit of study and practice, as with any language. And if you're a visitor, especially if you're on holiday, you've almost certainly got more interesting things to do than sit for hours poring over a textbook. But what if you could manage, *with very little effort*, to get quite a lot of Welsh place names completely right, and almost all the others near enough right so that the Welsh people you meet will know which place you're talking about? This book *Pronouncing Welsh Place-names* by Tony Leaver, 152 pages A4; £4.50 (Gwasg Carreg Gwalch) will show you how to do that.

Your easiest option is the list of Instant Welsh Place Names at the back of the book. It contains most of the well-known Welsh place names and quite a few not so well known. After each name in this list you'll find the pronunciation written out as near as it can be in English spelling. For example, the pronunciation of Ystradgynlais is given as *usstradd-gun-lice.* If you read this off just as if it was a string of English words, you'll have almost exactly the correct Welsh sound of the name. In some cases the English spelling will be close to the correct Welsh sound but slightly off beam in places, as with *mack-unth-leth* for Machynlleth.

But you won't find in this list all the Welsh words you might want to pronounce, and the list won't help you to recognise these words when other people say them. So the rest of the book is designed to introduce you to Welsh pronunciation in general. And you'll be surprised how easy it is.

Welsh spelling, unlike English spelling, is extremely tidy and regular and the rules are mostly very simple and logical. Once you know the rules, you can pronounce almost any Welsh word correctly on sight. And most of the sounds you find in Welsh words are the same, or as near as makes no difference, as sounds we have in English.

Take our old friend Betws-y-coed. The trick here is to know that the 'w' is pronounced like an English 'oo'. If you say *bettooss a koid,* sounding it just as if it was a string of English words, then you'll have almost exactly the correct Welsh pronunciation. There's nothing there that needs a longer than average tongue, and there's nothing there that breaks the standard Welsh spelling rules.

It's true, of course, that there are a few difficult sounds in Welsh names – the famous 'll', for example – but there's no law that says you have to get them 100% right. People who weren't brought up to speak English often have trouble with 'th' and say things like 'What eez zeess?' for 'What is this?', but that doesn't stop English people from understanding them. In this book you'll have the option of either learning these hard sounds or finding ways of fudging them – it's up to you.

So why not have a go? You never know, you might surprise yourself next time you're doing a commentary on your holiday video of Penrhyndeudraeth.

Key to symbols

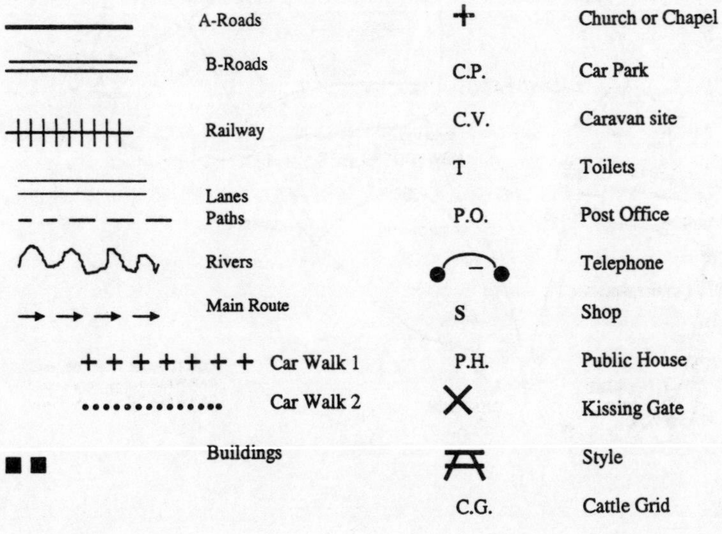

———	A-Roads	+	Church or Chapel
═══	B-Roads	C.P.	Car Park
┼┼┼┼┼┼┼┼	Railway	C.V.	Caravan site
═══	Lanes	T	Toilets
– – – – –	Paths	P.O.	Post Office
∿∿∿	Rivers		Telephone
→ → → →	Main Route	S	Shop
+ + + + + + +	Car Walk 1	P.H.	Public House
....	Car Walk 2	✕	Kissing Gate
■ ■	Buildings		Style
		C.G.	Cattle Grid

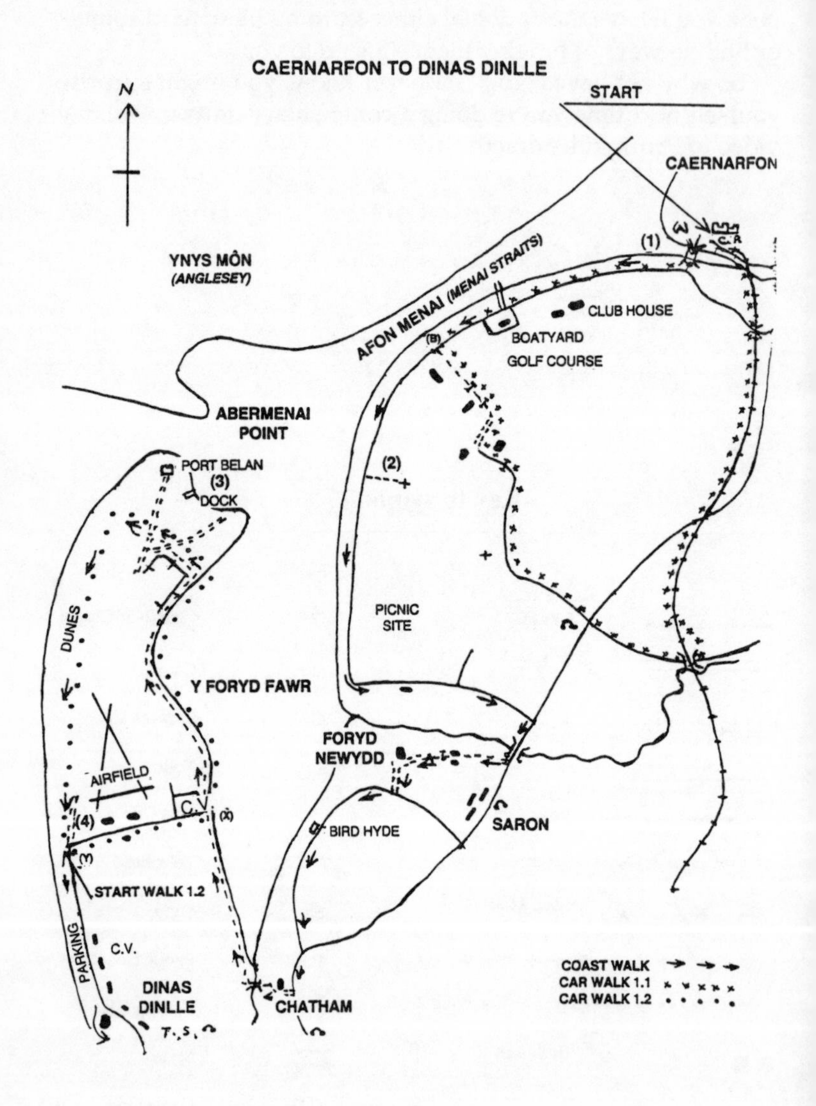
CAERNARFON TO DINAS DINLLE
N
START
CAERNARFON
C.R
(1)
YNYS MÔN
(ANGLESEY)
AFON MENAI (MENAI STRAITS)
CLUB HOUSE
BOATYARD
GOLF COURSE
ABERMENAI
POINT
PORT BELAN
(3)
DOCK
(2)
PICNIC
SITE
DUNES
Y FORYD FAWR
FORYD
NEWYDD
AIRFIELD
C.V
(4)
SARON
BIRD HYDE
START WALK 1.2
PARKING
C.V.
DINAS
DINLLE
CHATHAM
COAST WALK
CAR WALK 1.1
CAR WALK 1.2

Walk 1 *11 miles*

Caernarfon - Y Foryd Fawr - Caer (Fort) Belan - Dinas Dinlle

OS Maps:	1:25 000 *Llŷn Peninsula East Explorer 13.*
Start:	Car park on harbour at foot of Caernarfon Castle.
Access:	Caernarfon can be reached by main line train to Bangor and then bus. The town is connected to the National bus network.
Parking:	On the harbour.
Grade:	Easy – level walk on roads or well maintained paths.

(-)	denotes Car walk
[-]	denotes Point of interest

Walk Directions:

(A) Crossing the harbour entrance by the modern swing bridge, we turn right along the road which follows the foreshore of Afon Menai *(Menai Straits)*. If we look back before the road bends left, we get a fine view of the castle **[1]** with it's unique polygonal towers and banded stonework, we can also see the town walls as well as a view up Afon Menai. This unfenced road, with wide grass verges, runs for three miles along the very edge of the straits and indeed can get flooded by the tide. After passing the golf club and a small boatyard, the southern entrance to the straits comes into view, with Trwyn Abermenai (Point) on the Ynys Môn side and Caer (Fort) Belan **[2]** on the other. **(B)** A little further along is a picnic site with views across Y Foryd Fawr towards the Belan peninsula. The bay dries out at low tide and is a well known site for wading birds.

We now have to follow the road inland for just under a mile

in order to cross Afon Gwyrfai, turning right at the T-junction. Immediately after crossing the bridge, we take the second of the two gates on the right, down a drive leading between a house on the left and farm buildings on the right. Passing through a couple of gates by the buildings, and keeping to the right of the next two fields over stiles, the path comes out on a farm track leading to Foryd Newydd farm. Passing through the farmyard and turning left down the driveway, we come out on a narrow road. Following this to the right, first passing Foryd Cottage and then a bird watching hide, we bear inland to reach another road in 200 yards. Turn right again and after another 200 yards there is a footpath on the right down what looks like a private drive to a house called Chatham. Following this path down behind the house; over a stile; down a farm track; and over another stile onto a path, we come to a footbridge over Afon Carrog at the head of Y Foryd Fawr. The path now bears right along the top of the dyke and after ¼ mile there is a caravan site, with a lane leading off to the left.

For those who perhaps feel that they have walked far enough for the first day, turning left down this lane (which becomes a tarmac road after the site) leads, in just under a mile, to the seafront where a left turn and a further mile brings us to Dinas Dinlle.**(X)** For the rest of us, we can carry on along the dyke for just under a mile until the footpath comes to an end with a rather curt notice to the effect that beyond is private land. Foryd Bay floods at high tide, but assuming this notice to mean the land within the fencing, it is possible to walk along the foreshore turning inland with the fence, soon to cross a lane and then another that leads to the entrance to Fort Belan.**[3]**

Following the fence line and making for the sand dunes, we get a good view of the entrance to Afon Menai from the high point. Considering the narrowness of the channel, the currents, and the turbulent waters over the bar, it is not surprising that so many sailing ships came to grief with a considerable loss of life. To the north-west is Ynys Llanddwyn with its lighthouse, ruined chapel and cottages. At one time the lifeboat that saved so many lives was stationed here.

We now turn south, taking one of the many paths through the dunes, and arrive back on the road that runs along the sea front, passing Caernarfon airport on the way. **[4] (Y)**

Dinas Dinlle, with its two mile stretch of sand, is a popular seaside hamlet with its fair share of caravan sites, beach shops and cafes. Dogs are banned from a third of the beach at the populated end, but they can of course be walked along the road where this restriction applies. There are a couple of small hotels, two or three cafes and shops, camping site, telephone and toilets, but it must be admitted that accommodation is limited.

Points of Interest:

[1] Our journey begins on the harbour beneath the towering ramparts of Edward I's mighty castle, built between 1283 and 1323 to impress and subdue the Welsh. The castle also houses the Regimental Museum of the Royal Welch Fusiliers.

A hundred or more years ago, Cei Llechi (the *Slate Quay*) where cars now park would have been covered with the products brought down from the vast quarries of the Nantlle area of Snowdonia.The harbour would have been crowded with sailing ships, many of which would have been built, owned and crewed by men from the peninsula – over two hundred were built here in Caernarfon – waiting to load for industrial Britain, the Continent and the Americas. Those bound for the latter would also have offered passage, albeit an uncomfortable one, to emigrants to the New World. On the return journey the ships would have brought back salt fish from Newfoundland, cotton from the United States and guano from South America.

For a detailed guide to this historical town, see: *Caernarfon: The Town's Story*, Michael Senior, (Gwasg Carreg Gwalch) £1.95.

[2] In a field on the left, is an interesting small church that can only be reached by a footpath. No longer in use, Llanfaglan church was renovated in the 18th century but has a lintel over the north doorway bearing a 5th/6th century Latin inscription.

[3] The fort was built in the 18th century. by Lord Newborough at his own expense, to guard the southern entrance to the Straits from the French during the Napoleonic wars. Although garrisoned by four hundred men, they were never called upon to fight.

The fort and associated dry dock is no longer open to the public. When it was, the cannons were fired for the amusement of the tourists. On one such occasion a projectile went through the sail of a passing yacht, landing on the beach on Ynys Môn, a tribute to the accuracy of the cannon, but frowned upon by the authorities. During the Second World War, patrol boats were based in the dock to guard the Straits and the coast down to the end of the Llŷn peninsula.

[4] This airfield was built in 1941 as RAF Llandwrog, where air gunners and navigators were trained. As a consequence the beach and dunes were heavily mined and remains of the defences can be found in the area. Alarmed at the number of air crashes in the mountains of Snowdonia the then medical officer formed a special unit for the search and rescue of aircrew. This became the first RAF Mountain Rescue Unit, which was to be copied elsewhere in the UK and overseas. Whilst their primary duty is to RAF personnel, they still provide valuable assistance to all in need in the mountains and at sea. To this day rescue helicopters from RAF Valley, across the bay on Ynys Môn, carry out this life saving work. The RAF moved from Llandwrog in 1945 and for many years it became derelict. Nowadays it is used for private flying. There is a small air museum, coffee bar and restaurant in the old control tower, and it is popular with visitors.

Over the years there have been hundreds of shipwrecks round the Llŷn peninsula, but we will refer to just a few of interest. Some of those wrecked in the 1700's were ships engaged on the notorious triangle run – taking manufactured goods from Liverpool to West Africa, slaves to America, and then cotton back to Liverpool. These were sailing ships, which were not easy to control; but with the arrival of the steamship the number of casualties fell off dramatically although the S.S.Timbo was lost in 1920. Perhaps the most bizarre wreck occurred in 1971 when an ex-wartime amphibious vehicle known as a D.U.K.W. was finally wrecked on the third attempt to sail to Australia.

Legend has it that Caer Arianrhod, a Celtic fort connected to the Mabinogion tales, was inundated at the northern end of the beach and that, at very low tide, stone remains can be seen. At the southern end of the beach, the hill directly in front bears the remains of an early coastal fort, Dinas Dinlle, half of which has been washed away by the sea. In the 3rdC. it was occupied by the Roman Legions and in the 20th by the British Army, as witness the concrete gun emplacement at its base!

For fuller details, see *Llŷn, The Peninsula's Story*, Michael Senior (Gwasg Carreg Gwalch) £1.95.

CAR WALKS:

1.1

Description:	Good views of Caernarfon Castle; a walk along Afon Menai *(Menai Straits)*; through lanes to return alongside a narrow gauge railway.
Distance:	5 miles.
Time:	2 hours 15 minutes
Going:	Easy.
Facilities:	All available in Caernarfon.
Start:	Caernarfon Castle.

Parking the car on the Slate Quay below the castle, join the main walk at the outset **(A)** and follow the directions along Afon Menai. Just beyond the golf club and a small boatyard **(B)**, there is a gate into what looks like the drive to a private house, with a kissing gate alongside. Follow the white painted stone lined path passed the house and through a gate into the front garden of another house. Keeping to the wall on the left, go through another gate into the back garden, and in front a small gate onto a narrow path which in a few yards opens into a much wider grass lane.

Go through the farm and bear left round the farmhouse onto a tarmac lane. Through a gate at the top of the hill, the road bears right with fine views over Afon Menai. Passing a chapel on the right the road starts to descend with views over lush farmland towards Snowdonia. Keep straight ahead at the crossroads and in ½ a mile, pass under the railway bridge. At the far side go through the gate on the left and up the incline to the rail track. After a few yards the path crosses the track to the cycleway, which it now becomes, and leads back to Cei Llechi and the car park.

This line is part of the old Welsh Highland Railway which ran from Caernarfon, through Snowdonia, to Porthmadog. It was abandoned many years ago and is now being restored. At present it runs for the 3 miles to Dinas, but will eventually be restored along its full length.

1.2

Description:	A WW2 airfield and museum; a walk along saltings to an 18th century fort; return through sand dunes.
Distance:	4¼ miles.
Time:	2 hours.
Going:	Easy.
Facilities:	Toilet at start; shops, cafes & toilets at south end of beach; refreshments at airport.
Start:	Dinas Dinlle (431 583).

Leaving Cei Llechi car park, turn right and follow the railway to a roundabout. Turn right and at the bottom of the hill take the road on the right signposted to Saron. Follow this road for 5 miles to the village of Llandwrog. Turn right at the T-junction in the village and ½ mile, turn right at the next T-junction. In ¾ mile, arrive at Dinas Dinlle and drive the mile to the far end of the beach. Park the car on the pebble area.

Now, walking down the straight road in front, passing the entrance to the airfield, carry on straight ahead to come out on the foreshore of Y Foryd Fawr. This is where we join the main walk at **(X)** and, turning left, follow these directions round the promontory to arrive back at the car. **(Y)**.

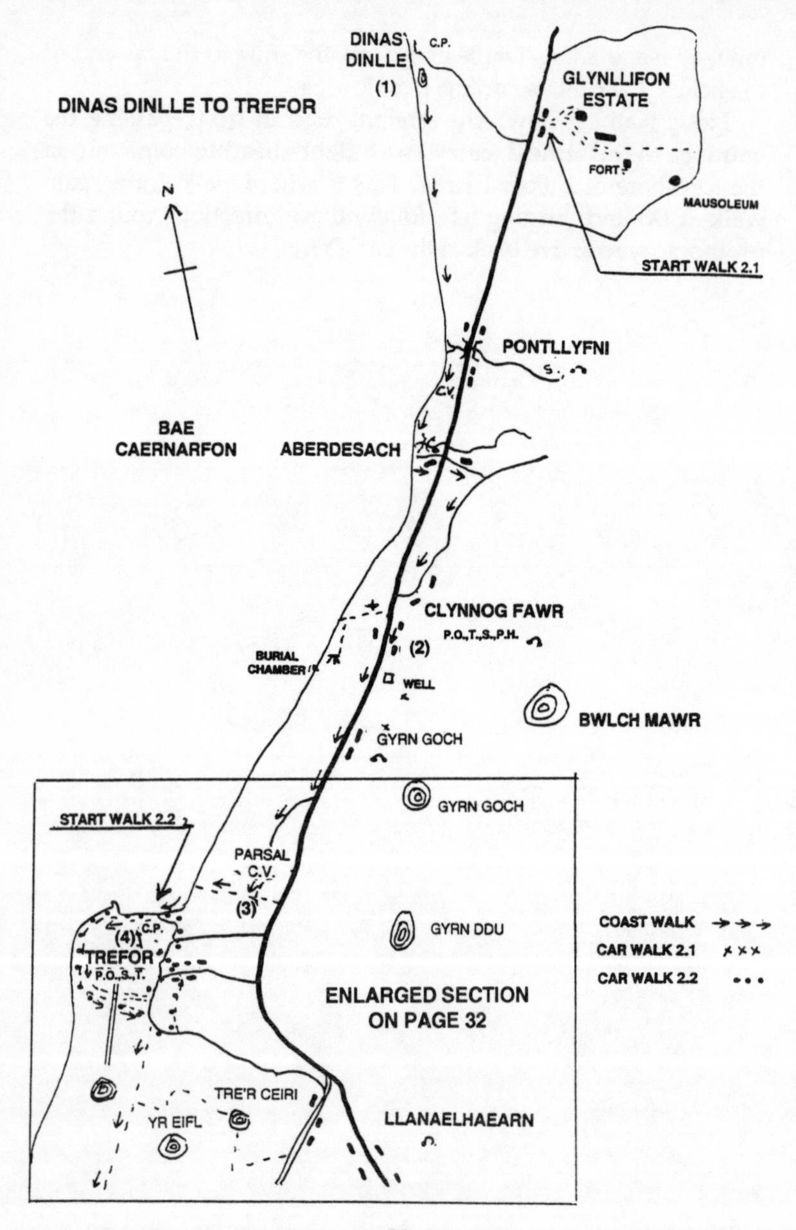
DINAS DINLLE TO TREFOR
DINAS
DINLLE
C.P.
(1)
GLYNLLIFON
ESTATE
FORT
MAUSOLEUM
START WALK 2.1
N
PONTLLYFNI
S.
C.V.
BAE
CAERNARFON
ABERDESACH
CLYNNOG FAWR
P.O.,T.,S.,P.H.
(2)
BURIAL
CHAMBER
WELL
BWLCH MAWR
GYRN GOCH
GYRN GOCH
START WALK 2.2
PARSAL
C.V.
(3)
C.P.
(4)
TREFOR
P.O.,S.,T.
GYRN DDU
ENLARGED SECTION
ON PAGE 32
TRE'R CEIRI
YR EIFL
LLANAELHAEARN
COAST WALK
CAR WALK 2.1
CAR WALK 2.2

Walk 2 *11 miles*

Dinas Dinlle - Aberdesach - Clynnog Fawr - Gyrn Goch - Trefor

OS Maps: 1:25 000 *Llŷn Peninsula East Explorer* 13
Start: Southern end of Dinas Dinlle Beach
Access: 2 miles off the A 499 at Glynllifon, which is on the bus route from Caernarfon to Pwllheli.
Parking: On the foreshore at southern end of beach.
Grade: Moderate: Seashore, country lanes and last section muddy in wet weather.

(-) denotes Car Walk
[-] denotes Point of Interest

Walk Directions:

This next section presents a problem in that, except in a few places, there is no path along the actual coast and although it is possible to walk along the beach for most part, it is very stony and therefore hard going. At low tide the sand is exposed in places. We have therefore chosen a combination of seashore and minor roads.

We start by going round the seaward side of the shop below the hill, passed the Second World War stone pillbox. At the far end of the stone wall, gain access to the path and steps leading up to the top of the hill. As mentioned previously, half of the fort has been eroded by the sea and it is still taking its toll, so beware of going too near the edge. **[1]**

We descend the hill by the obvious path in front which, after a couple of fields, drops down to the beach. Progress at the back of the beach for the next two miles, to Pontllyfni, is not too bad, there being a path for the last ¼ mile. The buildings over the fence from here are a fish farm. At low tide it is possible to wade across Afon Llyfni, but if this is not the case then follow the waymarked path up river for ¼ mile to the road bridge, and return down the opposite bank. Following the bay round, we come to a lane and small caravan site and, crossing the green with the standing stone in front, drop down onto the stony beach. Shortly, rounding Trwyn Maen Dylan, the three peaks of Yr Eifl come dramatically into view. The going gets easier now, there being a grassy path leading, after passing a row of holiday chalets and crossing a bridge, to the beach at Aberdesach. **(2)** There is a good stretch of sand here with picnic tables and seasonal toilets.

To avoid further walking on stones take to the road from here – the slight extra distance is more than compensated by the speed of progress. Passing between the cottages, cross the main road, which is busy, narrow, and without footpath; go up the narrow lane opposite, turning right at the T-junction in a ¼ mile. In just over a mile this lane drops down into the village of Clynnog Fawr, which was an important stopping place for pilgrims. For today's travellers it has three hotels, shop/P.O. and toilets.**[2]** The next ½ mile is difficult because the road is busy and there is no footpath but after this the road has been widened and there is a good grass verge – and even a pavement passed the cottages at Gyrn Goch. Just under two miles after leaving Clynnog Fawr, where the road widening ends, thankfully take the narrow road on the right. ½ mile down the lane, after passing several cottages, there is a turning on the right that leads into Parsal farm and caravan site. Passing through several gates in the farmyard we keep straight on passed the caravans, through a boat park, onto a rough farm track across a field, through another gateway and alongside a little stream, to arrive at a wooden foot bridge. Crossing the field to the gate opposite and following round the left of the next field come to another bridge in the corner, and again keeping to the left make for the gap in the far corner.**[3]**

Now we have a decision to make; although this path has

recently been opened up and waymarked, it is extremely muddy and only provides difficult access to the beach. [It is suggested that in very wet weather, especially when the tide is high, it would be prudent to seek an easier route in which case, having passed through the gap and over a stream we turn left through a gate making, across a couple of fields, towards the farmhouse of Cefn-buarddau (OS 385467), the drive to which leads onto the main road. Turn right on the main road and in 100 yards turn right again down the ½ mile straight road. At the bottom of this road, we take a sharp right turn at the walled grass triangle, and this narrow lane leads down to the harbour car park.] For the direct route, turn right after passing through the gap and over the stream and, keeping the stream down on the right, make for the small gate in front (not the larger gate slightly left). From here on it is very muddy and very slippery, but the path is waymarked down to the beach. The object then is to walk the short distance along the beach to the harbour car park; but before crossing the stile onto the beach, check the state of the tide to make sure that it is possible to get round the outcrop of clay to the left. If this doesn't look possible then we must try to follow the line of the fence until we reach a point, in 50 yards or so, where the beach is accessible. Serious erosion is taking place and the underlying soil is clay into which, in places, it is possible to sink over boot tops so care is needed. 100 yards along the beach we come to the car park. There are seasonal toilets here and an interesting information board. There is also a board warning of soft mud – a fact of which we will be well aware! **(X) [4]**

Crossing through the gate at the base of the pier, we follow the dirt road round, and over a bridge, for 100 yards. We then take the rough path that appears to lead round the low headland in front, but which in fact peters out at the remains, of an old pier. It is necessary to climb the fence on the left so as to gain access to the grass path round the headland. This does not seem to be an official path but it is obviously well used – and this is not surprising since the cliff scenery is magnificent; but take care, as the unfenced cliff edge is a 50 foot drop to the rocks below. After a little over ½ a mile or so there is another fence to be negotiated, and then we head towards the white cottages, known as West End, passing in front on the grass path that then bears left, inland. After passing through the next gate, and just before the farm, there is a path on the left that takes us up behind the farmyard onto the dirt access road. From here, the size of the quarry can be fully appreciated; its concrete crushing and grading plant resembling some medieval Spanish fortress. Carrying on along this path, the high stone wall on the left hides what used to be the manager's house, which is now the only hotel in the village. Shortly after the hotel entrance, the dirt road passes under the quarry incline and continues straight ahead into the village: if this is not your wish, then take the overgrown path immediately on the right, which doubles back onto the incline; but just before doing so there is a kissing gate on the left. Crossing diagonally to the stile in the far corner, and then keeping to the bottom edge of this field we come out, over a stile, onto a steep narrow lane where we turn right. **(Y)**

Apart from the hotel mentioned there is only the odd B&B for accommodation. The village has a cafe, P.O., shop, phone, toilets and is on a bus route.

Points of Interest:

[1] The views from the top of Dinas Dinlle are exceptional; to the north are Afon Menai and Caernarfon, which for the Romans would have been within signalling distance of their main fort at Segontium; to the east are the mountains of Snowdonia, with Snowdon itself the right hand one of the two peaks in the distance. At times, the smoke from the little train going up the mountain can be seen quite clearly. There are fourteen peaks over 3,000 feet in the range.

For further information: *The Gods and Heroes of North Wales*, Michael Senior (Gwasg Carreg Gwalch) £3.

[2] The church, dedicated to St Beuno, is well worth a visit and its importance on the pilgrim route is shown by its size.

Founded in the 7th century. the present church was built in the l6th century. and the saint is reputed to be buried in the little chapel connected to the main church by a covered passageway. To be seen: a very early stone sundial; a massive dugout chest to hold contributions for the pilgrims; a pair of dog tongs for removing same from the church. Although usually referred to as the pilgrims route, it is also known as the Saints' Way. For those who haven't seen one before there is a good example of a Neolithic burial chamber – a large capstone balanced on three, or, in this case, four uprights – ½ mile down the lane on the south side of the churchyard. There is also access to the beach down this lane but again it is very stony, and recourse to the road is recommended. 300 yards down the main road, set back on the left, is St Beuno's well where pilgrims refreshed themselves.

[3] We are now entering quarrying country: just as the slate quarries of Snowdonia roofed industrial Britain, so the granite quarries of the Llŷn paved the streets. All the quarries have long since closed and nature has hidden the worst scars. Looking up to the left we can see the line of the incline coming down from the quarry on the slopes of Gyrn Goch mountain and we are about to pass over it as it would have carried on to a wooden jetty now washed away. There is now a close-up view of Yr Eifl and the village of Trefor nestling below the huge quarry. There is no way round the seaward side of the mountain and in the next stage we will have to follow the pilgrims and climb up to the col between the centre and right-hand peaks – a climb of 1,100 feet. Had quarrying not stopped when it did the latter peak would no longer be there since, as we shall see later, it was being attacked from both sides. On the summit of the left-hand peak, Tre'r Ceiri is what is considered to be one of the finest examples of an Iron Age hill fort. The massive outer walls and gateways are clearly seen, as are the foundations of the 150 or so round huts within. Certain restorative work is currently being carried out by Cadw, the authority responsible for historic buildings in Wales.

[4] The village is dominated by the quarry, its raison d'être, and was named by Samuel Holland after his foreman, Trefor Jones. The quarry opened in 1850 and closed in 1971. It produced granite setts for paving streets in the towns and chippings for tarmacadam roads. The stone was brought down the incline to the pier in front which was built in 1869 and extended with a wooden jetty in 1912 so that ships had access at all states of the tide. At one time there was a large reinforced concrete hopper on the pier, said to be the first such structure in Wales. Fortunately this eyesore was demolished in 1986. The granite is of a particularly fine quality and when polished is still in demand as architectural stone. They also still produce blanks for curling stones.

CAR WALKS:

2.1

Description:	An interesting country park walk. Although Glynllifon is not part of our coast walk, the Newborough family, whose estate this was, have a long connection with the peninsula. One member of the family built Fort Belan, another is buried on Ynys Enlli the pilgrim's route to which passed through the estate. The house is not open to the public but the grounds and outluing buildings are well worth a visit.
Distance:	2 miles.
Time:	1½ plus.
Going:	Easy. Some of the paths are designed for wheelchairs.
Facilities:	Café, toilets, shop, children's play area.
Start:	Glynllifon. (454 553)

Glynllifon lies on the A499, 5 miles south of Caernarfon and 15 miles north of Pwllheli. Passing under the entrance archway take the road to the left to the car park.

The buildings in front form part of the estate workshops dating back to the mid 19th century. Amongst the various items of interest is the old steam engine restored by Fred Dibner. All the trades necessary for the maintenance of the estate are represented here.

Leaving the workshops follow the waymarked road over the bridge, with the old mill on the right, and then bearing left, pick up the asphalt path through the bushes and trees, passing the tiny boathouse and then a fine view of the house itself, built between 1836 and 1848. Continue up the asphalt path, passing on the right the stone remains of a children's play watermill, and then when the path finishes turn left over the bridge and then right up the other side of the river. Shortly, on the right, is the slate built amphitheatre where concerts are sometimes given. Continue up this path and turn right back over the river where the sign directs to 'George's Path'. Going up the rise in front pass a commemorative plaque by George Wright of the T.U.C. to those connected with the slate mining industry and at the top a large sculpture depicting this. There is also a small pond with an arm and hand rising from it's centre!

Bear right here and follow the path round the edge of the wood to arrive at a gate in a stone wall. Passing through this turn right and just passed a picnic table right again along a path which leads to a small octagonal building up in front, known as the Hermitage, where burial services were held for the family pets. Just before this edifice turn left over a stone bridge and follow this path round for 500 yards to come out on open fields with Fort Williamsbourg in front.

Going up the path between the fields enter the fort through a gate and tunnel in the curtain wall. Bear left and right through another short tunnel then, turning right, find another longer, narrower tunnel leading up to the tower. The fort was never intended to be used in anger as was Fort Belan, but rather as a folly for practising military exercises. It may be possible to climb the narrow circular staircase up to the first floor room of

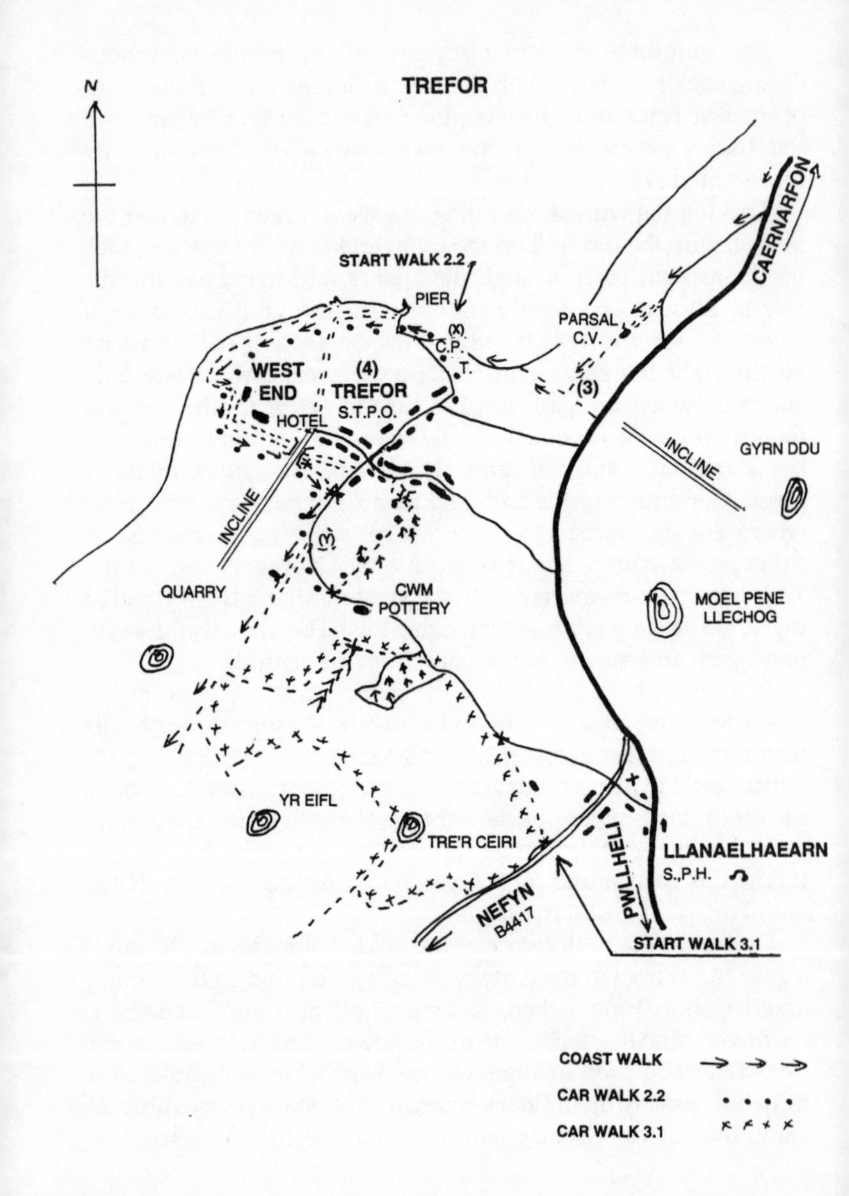

TREFOR
N
START WALK 2.2
PIER
(X)
C.P.
T.
PARSAL
C.V.
(3)
CAERNARFON
WEST
END
(4)
TREFOR
S.T.P.O.
HOTEL
INCLINE
GYRN DDU
INCLINE
(3)
QUARRY
CWM
POTTERY
MOEL PENE
LLECHOG
YR EIFL
TRE'R CEIRI
LLANAELHAEARN
S.,P.H.
PWLLHELI
NEFYN
B4417
START WALK 3.1
COAST WALK
CAR WALK 2.2
CAR WALK 3.1

the tower from where there are good views. The staircase up to the roof appears to be unsafe.

Returning now through the tunnel, turn right and leave the fort by another gate in the curtain wall. Turn half right up to a kissing gate onto a fenced path that leads back to the wood and so back down to the workshops and car park.

2.2

Description:	A tour round a purpose built quarry village ; some fine cliff scenery; glorious views and finally a shady walk by a stream.
Distance:	3¾ miles.
Time:	2 hours.
Going:	Moderate.
Facilities:	Shops, café, P.O. & toilets in village.
Start:	Trefor harbour (375 473).

Leaving the previous walk at Glynllifon turn left onto the A499 and travel south for 7¼ miles. Turn right down the secondary road signposted Trefor. At the bottom turn right by the triangular island onto the narrow road that leads down to the beach and car park. This is the point **(X)** where we join our coastal walkers and follow their directions to the end of the chapter **(Y)**.

Having crossed the stile and turned right up this narrow steep road keep on for 300 yards where a sharp left bend marks the high point of this walk. There are magnificent views back up the coast to Caernarfon. Carry on a further 200 yards to a kissing gate on the left. Bear half right across the field to another kissing gate in the far corner. It becomes rather wet here with no distinct path through the rushes, but out of the trees there is a low wooden plank over one of the worst parts and then heading slightly right to an oak tree with a footpath sign high up another low footbridge. Follow the fence down beside the wood with the stream babbling on the right. Through another kissing gate head down to the white cottage in front. Pass directly in front of this typical Welsh hill cottage to a slate footbridge and metal gate. Go straight across the field to a gate stile in the far corner and keeping to the right of this field negotiate another gate stile and in a few yards cross a wooden footbridge onto a path beside the river which, in 100 yards, comes out onto the main street.

Turn left and in the centre of the village follow the road round to the right. In ¼ mile arrive back at the little triangle and fork left to follow the road back to the car park.

Trefor - Yr Eifl - Nant Gwrtheyrn - Pistyll – Nefyn

OS Maps:	1:25 000 *Llŷn Peninsula East Explorer* 13 1:25 000 Llŷn Peninsula West Explorer 12
Start:	Trefor Harbour
Access:	1 mile off the A 499 north of Llanaelhaearn which is on the bus route from Caernarfon to Pwllheli.
Parking:	Trefor Harbour.
Grade:	Strenuous: Long climbs and rough underfoot.
(-)	denotes Car walk
[-]	denotes Point of interest

Walk Directions:

The previous two sections having been fairly easy, we now come to probably the most energetic part of the whole walk. As mentioned before there is no way we can get round the seaward side of the mountain and must therefore climb to the saddle between the two peaks in front, a fairly stiff climb of 1,000+ feet.

From the centre of the village we take the road with the signs for the Plas yr Eifl Hotel, but after 100 yards or so by the de-restriction sign and a patch of grass with a seat keep to the road up left rather than right to the hotel. This is a steep narrow lane and after 200 yards the path comes in on the right where those who opted out of the village now join the main route which continues up the lane for a further 300 yards. Here the lane turns sharp left but we continue straight on up what is now a grass lane leading to a derelict cottage, just beyond

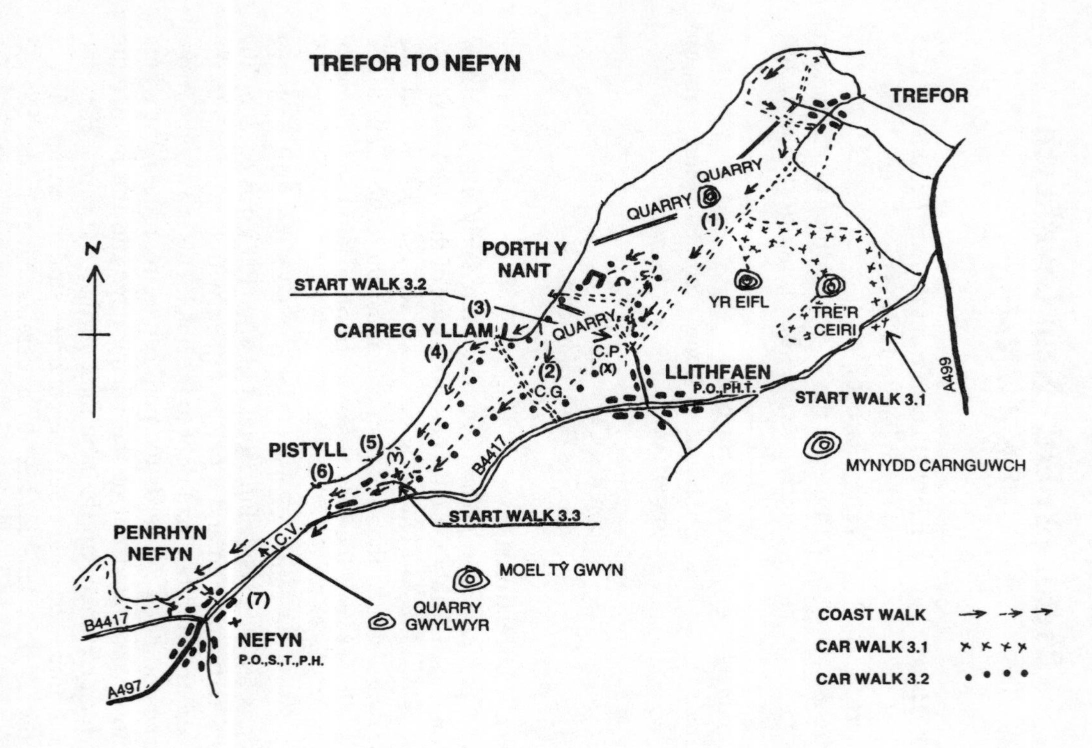
TREFOR TO NEFYN
N
TREFOR
QUARRY
QUARRY
(1)
PORTH Y
NANT
START WALK 3.2
(3)
CARREG Y LLAM
(4)
QUARRY
C.P.
(X)
(2)
C.G.
YR EIFL
TRE'R
CEIRI
LLITHFAEN
P.O.,PH.T.
START WALK 3.1
A499
MYNYDD CARNGUWCH
B4417
PISTYLL
(5)
(6)
START WALK 3.3
PENRHYN
NEFYN
C.V.
MOEL TŶ GWYN
QUARRY
GWYLWYR
(7)
B4417
NEFYN
P.O.,S.,T.,P.H.
A497
COAST WALK
CAR WALK 3.1
CAR WALK 3.2

which we pass through a gate onto the open mountainside. The path now roughly follows the line of the electricity poles up to the top of the pass. Now is the time to look back and get a bird's eye view of where we have walked over the past couple of days.**(A)**

Those who wish to explore the remains of the Iron Age fort on Tre'r Ceiri, and it is well worth a visit if you have the energy, will see a definite path on the left leading up through the heather to the top of the highest of the three peaks, but before reaching the steep part of this path another one goes off to the left round the shoulder of the mountain. It is then a matter of following the sheep tracks across the valley and entering the fort through the double walls of the western gateway, a distance of just under a mile.**(B)** Return by the same route or round the other side of the main mountain.**[1]**

We now descend from the pass down the rough stone road and shortly a view down the length of the peninsula comes into sight. Carrying on down this rough road we arrive at the car park **(X)** at the head of the valley, in the far corner of which, by the information board, is a path leading into the woods, well waymarked, and which shortly comes out at a picnic site on the now metalled road down to the village. Turning down the road there is a track into the trees on the right; this is part of the original pathway and joins the new road further down, where, just after a hairpin bend to the left, there is another waymarked path into the trees on the right. This newly made path leads along the base of the high escarpment and then, bearing left, follows the stream which separates the forest from the fields. Across the fields, beneath Cae'r Nant quarry is a small copse about which is another legend, namely that of a young girl who, on her wedding day, ran off to hide, as was the custom, only to be found by her lover a year later trapped in a hollow tree.

The path eventually comes out in the resident's car park at the rear of the village and turning right, passed the chapel, we arrive at the centre. There is an information office; cafe; toilets;

and phone. Passing to the left of the cafe the well defined path leads down to the beach at the bottom of the incline from Porth y Nant quarry.

There are two ways in which to proceed from this point:

(1) A higher route which follows the footpath shown on the O.S. and the path of the pilgrims, as far as Pistyll.

(2) A lower route along the beach and then on to Pistyll through N.T. land, keeping closer to the sea. There is little to choose between the two routes; the former is more strenuous but gives better views whilst the latter is nearer to our aim of keeping as close to the sea as possible, and could be more interesting to those 'into' quarries. Whichever route is chosen look out for herds of wild goats which inhabit this area.

(1) From the beach, where at one time there was a wooden jetty, we take the waymarked steps up the bank, passed the old machinery, through the bracken and where another path comes in from the left our path bears off to the right diagonally up the hillside making for an obvious steady climb to the top.**[2]** Carrying on up the slope we arrive at what is a typical 18th century Welsh farmhouse, Ciliau Isaf, and there is a stile on the left just before the outbuildings where the path goes behind the house to join the farm access track. After crossing a cattle grid we join a wider rough road that serves the quarry and two houses below. Across the way we take the stile signposted to Nefyn and keeping to the right of the field pass through a gate onto another farm lane. (The stile here only seems to serve the vegetable patch!). On entering the farm we take the gate passing into the cut grass in front of the cottage, leaving through another gate in front onto a short lane leading into a field, aiming for the clump of trees on the skyline. Keeping the fence on the right climb the stile at the far side and head slightly right to the brow of the hill in front from where the stile into the next field comes into view. We carry on along this path,

keeping to the right of the clump of trees and Cefnydd farm before crossing a stile onto open headland. Hereabouts are remains of a hospice that catered for the pilgrims at this, what might be called a staging post, on the route to Ynys Enlli. Dropping down the hill we cross a stile onto a metalled lane where on turning right we come to the tiny church of St Beuno.**[5]**

(2) For this route we carry on along the beach to Carreg y Llam quarry at the far end.**[3]** From behind the grading plant and hopper at the base of the pier steps and a steep path lead up the cliff. At the top of the climb we bear right and after crossing a stream and then a circular stone gate post we join what was the main access road where there is a small stone hut. Here we bear up left rather than going straight on to the quarry face. At the top of this grass slope, just before the warning signs, there is a stile on the left leading onto N.T. land.**[4]** Continuing alongside the fence on the right the path now descends a grass defile with views across to the magnificent twin bays of Porth Nefyn and Porthdinllaen. At the bottom, passing through a gateway and crossing a small ford we follow the obvious path which keeps to the landward side of the fields, below the bracken covered hillside. This path then brings us out at Pistyll church to join the others.**(Y)[5]**

Leaving the church we keep to the right with a pond on the left, cross the bridge and then bear left between the circular gate posts which brings us to the large Victorian mansion on the right – Plas Pistyll, built for a Mr. Goddard of silver polish fame. Last used as an hotel it has been empty for some years and fast becoming derelict. Going through the kissing gate in front we keep to the wall of the Plas and at the far side of the field, ignoring the newer stile on our right take the makeshift one in front.**[6]**

Crossing over the concrete road by the two stiles we bear right towards a gap in the broken wall in front. Following the path on the top of this wall over a stile, then through the bracken, keeping to the higher side we make for, but don't go through, the gate in the top left hand corner of the field. (Ignore the stile in the bottom corner). By the gate, through a gap in the hedge in front is a stile and bridge. More or less straight across the field we come to a group of derelict stone buildings and passing through them a stile. Keeping to the left of this field and passing the backs of the cottages we emerge onto the road by a lay-by.

Unfortunately we now have to follow this narrow stretch of road for ½ mile downhill until, immediately beyond the caravan site entrance on the right, there is a waymarked path to the beach. Just after we started down this road there is, set into the base of the wall on the left, an ancient church boundary stone which the pilgrims would have noticed. This path to the beach follows the line of the incline down from the quarry above to a long gone wooden pier. ½ mile along the beach, just before the sea defence rocks start, there are steps and path up the cliff leading into Nefyn. (Those who don't wish to visit the village can carry on along the beach gaining access to the cliff top by a path that runs in front of the modern flat roofed house by the little harbour). Dogs are not allowed on this part of the beach so during the season must leave the shore at this point. At the top of the cliff we can either proceed straight ahead along a path that comes out at the fire station at the bottom of the main street, or, turning right follow the path round to an unmade road which, on turning right again, leads to the top of the proper road down to the beach.[7]

With a population of 2,500 all facilities are available but the only bank (Midland) is now open mornings only.

Points of Interest:

[1] The landscape which one would expect to be flat, is seen to be covered with conical hills. Down below on the right is Nant Gwrtheyrn or, as it is sometimes known, Vortigern's valley since legend has it that he fled here to escape his enemies, Hors and Hengist in 450 AD. Overlooking the sea in the valley is Porth y Nant, a quarry village of some 24 houses, shop and

chapel, built in 1863 to house the workers in the three quarries, the remains of which can clearly be seen. Although the quarries, which opened in the mid 19th.C. closed in the 1930's the last inhabitants finally left in 1959 and the village became derelict until, in 1978, it was restored and turned into a National Language Centre for the teaching of Welsh. In its heyday, with the three quarries working and ships loading granite at the three jetties it must have been a vastly different place to today. Since the only access to the village was down a very steep rough track, supplies were brought in and shoppers taken out by ship so that, to some, Liverpool would be more familiar than Pwllheli! Another legend associated with the valley refers to the three curses laid on the inhabitants by the monks, that no son and daughter of the valley would marry each other; that there will never be any hallowed land; that the valley will live and die three times; all of which have so far come true!

[2] The area we pass through is one of Special Scientific Interest, being a fine example of an exposed coastal woodland featuring stunted oaks and birch trees with blackthorn and hawthorn lower down where the underlying soil is clay.

[3] This is a very good example of an early 20th.C. quarry with its now derelict pier and associated buildings. The quarry, although closed in 1963, is still private property and any exploring is at ones own risk - it can be a dangerous place.

[4] This is Carreg y Llam which rises a sheer 300 feet from the sea and is another S.S.S.I. It is an important nesting site for thousands of sea birds, particularly guillemots, razorbills and kittiwakes but since these are on the exposed north west side of the rock only visible by boat. Access to the rock is dangerous. Archaeologists have found remains of a fort on this site.

[5] St Beuno founded the church in the 7th.C. and may have been laid to rest here under the altar stone. Alterations have obviously taken place over the centuries, the original wood and plaster being replaced by a Celtic stone building and the thatched roof being replaced 150 years ago. During restoration in 1949 the remains of a l4th.C. mural on a plaster of beef fat and lime, was found. The font is Celtic and water from a holy well nearby is still used for baptisms. Of the three windows one was for lepers. There is no electricity and on Christmas Eve it is lit by candles and the floor strewn with rushes and wild herbs - quite an experience. Amongst the many interesting headstones is that of Rupert Davies, the actor known for his portrayal of Maigret in the T.V. of that name who lived in the parish. The pilgrims were accommodated in the hospice on the hill behind or the nearby monastery and tenants of what is now Pistyll farm were obliged to supply sustenance to pilgrims who asked, in lieu of rent. Medieval herbs can still be found growing in the churchyard.

[6] The stile on the right incidentally, leads down to Pistyll bay and to a narrow quay built into the rocks at Penrhyn Bodeilas at the south end of the bay where there is a small quarry. In 1839 the brig *Sapho* was wrecked near here and the captain gave each of his crew two sovereigns to be sewn into their jackets to pay for their burial. All were lost save an apprentice who was found in a treacle barrel. They are buried in Nefyn church. Recently an 10 acre field disappeared into the sea here.

[7] Edward 1 held a tournament here in 1284 to celebrate his conquest of Gwynedd and the Black Prince granted the town a charter in 1355. At that time there was a large herring industry and the town insignia is three herrings. In 1747, 5,000 barrels of herrings were exported. Nefyn has for long played a leading roll in the maritime history of the peninsula from the early days of building ships to the present day sea captains and this history is admirably displayed in a museum housed in the old church, with its sailing ship weather vane. (Unfortunately only open during the height of the season). Over 100 ships were built on the beach at the far end of the bay, the last being the schooner *Venus*, 107 tons, in 1880. This activity required, apart from shipwrights, blacksmiths, sailmakers, ropemakers etc., numerous taverns for it was thirsty work! Since most of the ships would be owned and sailed by locals this led to the teaching of navigation and the establishment of insurance companies (Clubs). Shares in vessels were offered in 64ths. and many of the locals would have had an interest.

CAR WALKS:

3.1

Description:	A visit to what is considered to be the finest example of an Iron Age fort; spectacular views.
Distance:	4 miles.
Time:	2½ hours.
Going:	Strenuous.
Facilities:	None.
Start:	½ mile west of Llanaelhaearn on the B4417 (380 444)

Almost at the top of the hill out of Llanaelhaearn on the B4417 there is a lay-by on the right. Leaving the car go through the kissing gate and head slightly right to a stile at the far side of the field. Keeping up slightly in the next field behind the smallholding come to a stile roughly half way along the fence in front. The path then descends down to a kissing gate on the narrow road below.

Turning left come to a small conifer wood on the left in ½ mile. A gateway leads up into the wood but turn right immediately on entering to follow a path just inside the trees to a stile which opens onto a field. Keeping the wall on the right, through a gate and then in 30 yards through a kissing gate where the main path descends, a rather indistinct path branches off left up the right hand flank of the grass spur. The path can be distinctly seen further on where it bears right and climbs steeply up a cleft in the rock. The path then levels out and bears right to meet that coming up to the pass from Trefor.

This is where we join the main coastal path but leave almost immediately to take the definite path on the left leading up to the summit of the central peak, but before reaching the steep part another narrower one will be seen going off to the left round the shoulder of the mountain. There is no distinct path now and it is a matter of finding a sheep track across the shallow valley towards the peak of Tre'r Ceiri and entering the settlement through the double walls of the western gateway.

Having examined the remains of the fort and admired the stunning views, leave by the southern gateway. Follow the, at first, steep but clear path down towards the wall in front but turn off left before reaching it on a path which swings round the base of the mountain to emerge on the road some 300 yards from where the car is parked.

3.2

Description:	A descent into a valley of legends to view the remains of what was once a thriving industrial community in Nant Gwrtheyrn; completing the circle with a pleasant walk through fields via a tiny pilgrim's church.
Distance:	5 miles.
Time:	3 hours.
Going:	Strenuous.
Facilities:	Café, toilet and phone in Porth y Nant; picnic site near car park.
Start:	½ mile north of the B4417 at Llithfaen. (354 440)

From the previous car park continue along the road towards Nefyn turning right at the cross roads in the centre of Llithfaen, the highest village in Llŷn. ½ mile on after passing a row of cottages, come to a car park on the left by a conifer forest.

This is where we join point **(X)** of the main walk and follow these directions down to the beach. At this point the main walkers have a choice but we follow the directions for the second alternative and carry on along the coast as far as St Beuno's church.**(Y)**

After leaving the church turn left on the metalled road and in a few yards take the wooden stile on the left. This path winds up the hillside but part way up take the path to the left (waymarked) rather than the wider path ahead. After passing over a stile and keeping alongside the wall on the right arrive at the top. Pause for breath and to admire the view back towards the twin bays of Nefyn and Morfa Nefyn. For this walk ignore the N.T. waymarker which points to the left and take the stile immediately in front to pass behind Cefnydd farm. Keeping the fence on the right pass through a couple of fields and over another stile into an open field. Bearing downhill and slightly right climb another stile and at the opposite side of the field enter a short grass lane leading, through a gate, onto what looks like the garden of the cottage in front but leave this by the gate to the right onto the farm access lane. Turn right and after a few yards left through a gate to follow the left hand side of the field up to another stile which leads out onto the rough quarry road.

Turn right and at a cattle grid take a path going up to the left which, at the top of the field, joins a bridleway coming in from the right. Follow this through a gate where the path becomes a little indefinite. However heading in the direction of Yr Eifl and first keeping a house down to the right and then the terrace of cottages up to the right emerge in the corner of the conifer forest by the car park.

Some may consider the two walks just described a little too ambitious for one day. There follows then a shorter, easier walk to replace walk 3.2.

3.3

Description:	A fairly gentle walk with good views and to end the tiny pilgrim's church at Pistyll.
Distance:	2 miles.
Time:	1 hour.
Going:	Moderate.
Facilities:	None.

Start: Pistyll church just off the B4417, 2 miles north of Nefyn. (329 423).

There is a N.T. car park just 50 yards down the small road leading to Pistyll church.

Cross the stile from the car park and take the zigzag path up the hill in front, following the N.T. waymarkers. At the top of the hill turn left and follow the fence round the headland with fine views down to Porth Pistyll with its disused tiny harbour at the south end of the beach, and across the bay to Porthdinllaen headland. After just under ½ mile the fence turns inland and although there is a N.T. waymarker the path is not too clear, but heading almost due north the path begins to descend passing through a gap with two or three wooden steps, in what remains of a low stone wall. A little further on another gap in a higher stone wall. Don't pass through but follow the arrow on this side of the wall to drop down to join the wide path coming in on the right from Nant Gwrtheyrn (part of walk 3.2. above). Carry on down this path, crossing a small ford, and then shortly through a gate on the right into a field. Make for the farm track in the bottom left hand corner and follow this along the edge of the fields and through two gates back to Pistyll church and the car park just up the road to the left.

Access to Pistyll beach can be gained by turning seawards at the second of the two gates mentioned above, where a steep path down to the shore will be found.

Walk 4 ***9 miles***

Nefyn – Porthdinllaen - Porth Tywyn - Tudweiliog

OS Maps:	1:25 000 *Llŷn Peninsula West Explorer* 12
Start:	Nefyn Square
Access:	Bus from Pwllheli.
Parking:	Quarter of mile on B4417 out of Nefyn
Grade:	Moderate: Some short sharp ups & downs and paths not always well maintained.

(-)	denotes Car walk
[-]	denotes Point of interest

Walk Directions:

Leaving the square on the Aberdaron road (B4417) notice, just before the new church and behind the public toilets an old lookout tower from which in days gone by it was possible to see the ships arriving and leaving Porth Nefyn. We take the second road on the right, opposite the school, **(A)** which leads to the beach, but before it starts to drop steeply follow the cliff top path round the wall of the castellated house on the left. The path looks down on the beach, where at one time, ships would unload their cargo into horses and carts and now holiday makers take advantage on the 1½ miles of sand to swim and sail.**[1]**

Above the tiny harbour a landslip has caused the path to be diverted through a kissing gate **(B)** onto what is a drive to a private house but after 50 yards a grass path leads out to the point from where there is a fine view of both bays. Returning on the other side of the point we pick up the cliff path again and follow this round the next bay for just under a mile where steps lead down to the road to the beach. **(X)** Our aim is the

NEFYN TO TUDWEILIOG

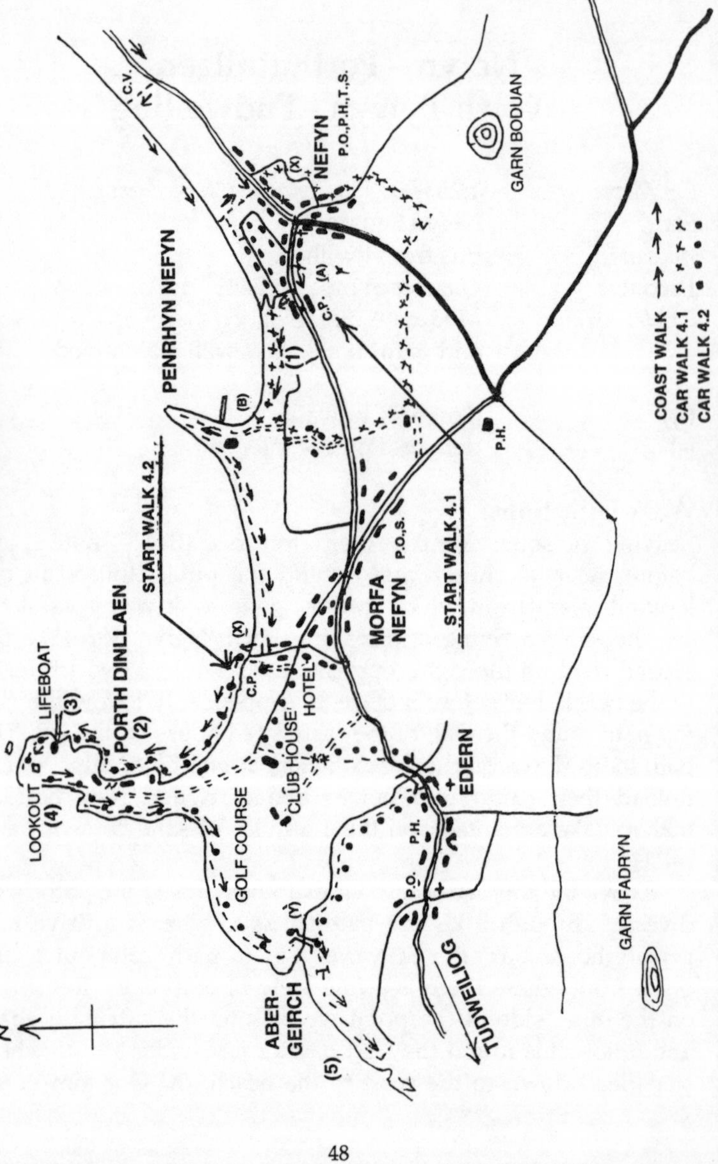

N
LOOKOUT
(4)
LIFEBOAT
(3)
PORTH DINLLAEN
(2)
START WALK 4.2
PENRHYN NEFYN
C.V.
GOLF COURSE
C.P.
(X)
(B)
ABER-
GEIRCH
(Y)
CLUB HOUSE
HOTEL
(1)
(X)
NEFYN
P.O.,P.H.,T.,S.
C.P.
(A)
(5)
MORFA
NEFYN
P.O.,S.
P.O.
P.H.
EDERN
START WALK 4.1
TUDWEILIOG
P.H.
GARN BODUAN
GARN FADRYN
COAST WALK
CAR WALK 4.1
CAR WALK 4.2

hamlet of Porthdinllaen **(4)** across the bay and, except at very high tide, the walk along the beach is very pleasant. Dogs are allowed on this section but not on the beach to the right.

[If the tide is unsuitable then take the steps up behind the toilets which emerge onto a car park at the top, where at the turn of the century there was a brick works with tall chimney. Crossing the car park, which incidentally belongs to the N.T. along with the coastline out to the point including the hamlet of Porthdinllaen, we turn right up the road to the golf club. Going through the gate in front the road leads across the course (beware of the golfers) and down to Porthdinllaen.]

At the bottom of the road there used to be a lime kiln on the right and a wooden jetty on the left. We follow the beach round passed the first house, Henblas, which at one time before it was burned down was a tavern called Tan-'rallt – the converted ships lifeboat at the side is not the result of a high tide! The corrugated iron building on piles in front was the Dora warehouse where the steamship of that name called once a week from Liverpool; she was sunk by a U-boat in 1917. Passing behind this building, which is now a holiday home, and a couple of others we cross the next beach to the tiny hamlet.**[2]**

Passing in front of the inn and cottages we go through the tiny courtyard and up a narrow passage which leads onto a path round the base of the cliffs. The old mooring eyes set into the rock and remains of the old breakwater can be seen. Following this path round the rocks we come to the next bay with the lifeboat station.**[3]** Crossing over the lifeboat slipway the little sandy cove makes an ideal spot to swim, but a set of steps in the corner of the breakwater lead up to the top of the cliff where a narrow track to the seaward side of the flagpole takes us out to the point. Here, on the rock outcrop offshore, there are usually to be seen basking seals. Continuing further round the headland we can take any of the grass paths that lead up to the now abandoned coastguard lookout.**[4]**

From here on the character of the coastline changes,

becoming more rugged with numerous rocky coves and some fine sandy beaches. We follow the edge of the golf course round the cliff top for about 1½ miles, passing an interesting fenced off blowhole on the way, until reaching the 5th. tee perched precariously on a promontory overlooking Aber-geirch (*Cable Bay*). At one time the telephone cable from Ireland came ashore here and at low tide it is sometimes possible to see remains of the cable. Don't go too close to the edge but follow the cliff round to a stile on the right just before the golfers green painted tin 'loo', and a scramble down the cliff takes us to the remains of the telephone terminal building on the beach. Old photographs show a tiny cottage built into the rock on the other side of the bay; the outlines of the foundations can just be seen. This is obviously not a suitable place to bathe.**(Y)** Crossing the wooden footbridge in front we head off right up the cliff to reach a gate at the top. Through this we are out on the open cliffs again with good views of the coast in front and behind. There is usually a fine display of wild flowers on the grassy cliff tops, particularly pink thrift and squill in early summer and a profusion of yellow iris on the banks of the many small streams that flow into the sea along this coast.

For the next 2½ miles there is little need of detailed instructions since the way ahead is obvious. Most fields have either a fence or remains of a wall on the seaward side and the path follows the fairly wide grassy headland outside these, over stiles, following the ups and downs of the path as it crosses little streams and visits a number of small coves.**[5]**

After this very pleasant 2½ mile walk we arrive at Porth Tywyn **(5)** where the two sandy coves between rocky headlands are the equal of any in Cornwall. The first is open to dogs but they are banned from the second more popular one. Those who have booked accommodation in Tudweiliog must now take the wide path to the farm passed the caravans. Going through the farmyard a well defined path leads, in ½ a mile to the village which has just one hotel, B&B. camping site, P.0./shop, phone and toilets. If accommodation is not available in the village it might be worth considering taking the bus back to your accommodation the previous night in Nefyn, just six miles down the road.

Points of Interest:

[1] The rounded hill inland is Garn Boduan on the summit of which is another Iron Age hillfort with the remains of 170 round houses and curtain walls. The woods thereabouts were once owned by Ann Boleyn and Elizabeth 1, whilst a little further inland, at Bodfel Hall, Dr Johnson's friend, Mrs. Thrale, was born.

[2] This collection of a dozen or so cottages and Tŷ Coch Inn was once a busy shipbuilding harbour with all the necessary workshops. Over 70 ships were built here, the last, in 1876, being the *Annie Lloyd,* a 149 ton brigantine. It is recorded that, in 1804, 700 vessels called here – 100 in one month – and a harbour master was appointed, a position which the lifeboat coxswain holds to this day though the duties are no longer so arduous albeit it is a popular port of call for visiting yachtsmen. In the mid 1800's, there was a proposal to make this tranquil spot the ferry terminal for Ireland. Fortunately the proposal was defeated by one vote in Parliament and Caergybi (Holyhead) became the port. The railway, which had already been built as far as Pwllheli, was extended no further and the building called Whitehall intended to be an hotel was not needed, although it was a tavern for some time. Smuggling was of course a major occupation with supplies coming in from Ireland, the Isle of Man and the Continent. At one time the supply of brandy was so great that the bottom dropped out of the market. The establishment of the coastguard in 1822 had little immediate effect.

[3] The lifeboat was established here in 1864 and has been kept busy ever since. A notable shipwreck was in 1881 when the captain of the Cyprian gave up his lifebelt to a young stowaway and lost his own life as a consequence.

[4] From here there is a panoramic view of the whole of Caernarfon Bay. The entrance to Afon Menai is 40 degrees East whilst the white lighthouse slightly to the left of that is Llanddwyn island mentioned in chapter 1. Holy Island, which is joined to mainland Ynys Môn (Anglesey) by a causeway, is clearly seen due north with the flashing light of South Stack lighthouse on the extreme western end. The tall chimney in the gap between Holy Island and Anglesey is that of the aluminium works, so placed to make use of the nearby Wylfa nuclear power station.

[5] Most of the coastal farms here had a cart track down to a cove for the collection of seaweed for the fields, stones for walls and paths, and possibly a fishing boat. Modern fertilisers and wire fencing have obviated the need for these tracks but they provide us with an easy way down to the shore.

The saddle back hill inland is Garn Fadryn and yes, it too has the remains of a hill fort. On a clear day, particularly in the evening, it is possible to see the Wicklow mountains south of Dublin. Still looking out to sea, it is not all that many years ago that there would always have been ships on the horizon, making their way round Anglesey to pick up the Liverpool pilot off Point Lynas. Fewer larger ships sail further out to sea and do not need a pilot. This as well as containerisation and better safety at sea has had its effect on beach combing which is not what it used to be unless one is an avid collector of plastic containers which are washed up on our shores in a vast range of shapes, sizes and colours, though some of the countries of origin give food for thought. (This is not always the case as the writer found on a recent visit to the Scillies, where the islanders were well supplied with clothing as a result of a container ship sailing straight into the Isles a year or two ago!) Another sign of the times is the number of low flying aircraft over the peninsula which come from the advanced flying school at RAF Valley on Anglesey.

CAR WALKS:
4.1

Description:	A pleasant cliff top walk and return to start through fields and lanes, with a look round the old maritime village of Nefyn.
Distance:	4 miles.
Time:	2 hours.
Going:	Easy but could be wet underfoot through the fields.
Facilities:	All available in Nefyn, Toilets & shop on road to beach.
Start:	Nefyn (305 405)

From the centre of Nefyn take the B4417 Aberdaron road and 200 yards after the war memorial there is a convenient car park on the left.

Leaving the car turn right out of the park back along the road and crossing take the first road on the left to the traeth (beach) which is where we join point **(A)** of the main walk. Follow these directions for the ½ mile round the bay to point **(B)** where, after passing through the kissing gate, turn left down the drive and right where it meets the narrow road. After 50 yards look out for a rough, narrow, overgrown lane on the left. This leads to a cluster of cottages round a pond. Follow the rough access road between the two cottages in front and in 100 yards or so come out onto the main road.

Crossing the road follow the footpath sign alongside the house directly opposite. Going straight ahead, through two kissing gates, over two wooden stiles and then a farm gate keep to the left of this field to find another kissing gate at the far end by the farm Tŷ Mawr. Keeping the farm on the right go through another gate beside the farm house and immediately turn left through a small rickety wooden gate down a narrow path which leads, after a few yards and an overgrown pond to another kissing gate and slate slab bridge. Keeping to the right of this field make for the stile at the far side and then bearing left enter a very overgrown farm lane which, after 100 yards, comes out onto the access lane to the farm on the left. Go through the gate immediately in front keeping to the left of the field to find a wooden stile in the corner. Negotiate this and immediately turn right to follow up the side of the field. Just beyond the house on the right go through a kissing gate onto the main road.

Turn left and after 50 yards cross to the lay-by on the opposite side. A yard or two further on go through a kissing gate on the right and head across the field with Garn Boduan directly in front keeping just to the right of the gorse patch. When the bottom of the valley comes into view veer off left down to the bottom where there are signs of a rough track leading across the wet valley and up the other side. Instead of crossing to the other side however look out for two or three shallow stone steps on the left up onto a low grass embankment by the finger post. Keep along the top of the embankment until a kissing gate is reached. Passing through don't take the path going up to the right but head towards the houses in front keeping to the right of the field. This is possibly the site of Edward's tournament in 1284. Another kissing gate leads onto a drive and then out onto the road.

Turn left into the village and after passing the Baptist chapel, the bakery and a row of cottages take the first street on the right. This leads through the old part of Nefyn to the old church with its distinctive sailing ship weather vane. The church is no longer used as such but has been turned into a very interesting maritime museum with particular emphasis on Nefyn and its seafaring tradition. Unfortunately the museum is only open during the main season.

Take the narrow street opposite the church entrance and then turn left on the main road through the village. Just before the mini-roundabout in the centre notice St Mary's well on the right; a never failing supply of water for pilgrims and villagers in days gone by. Turning right see the old look out tower on the right just before the new church. Continue along the road passed the village hall, war memorial and school to arrive back at the car park.

4.2

Description:	A walk across the sands to a pub on the beach; a chance to inspect a lifeboat and to look for seals; a brisk breezy cliff top walk with panoramic views and return by a pretty stream and fields.
Distance:	4½ miles.
Time:	2½ hours.
Going:	Moderate but a short rougher section over rocks and the stream section could be muddy.
Facilities:	Pub and toilets at both start and Porthdinllaen. Shop and pub in Edern.
Start:	Morfa Nefyn (282 407)

Leaving Nefyn car park drive the mile to Morfa Nefyn. At the diagonal crossroads fork right and in ½ mile just passed the Linksway hotel find a N.T. car park on the right at the bottom of the golf approach road. Park at the far end where there is a good view of the bay and descend by the steps in the corner to the beach.

Joining here the coast route **(X)** follow the main directions for the next 2½ miles until reaching point **(Y)** where, after crossing the footbridge turn left up the left bank of the river (i.e. the right bank facing up stream). Keep alongside the stream for the next ½ mile. In spring there is a profusion of yellow iris in the valley, followed by foxgloves and other wild flowers. Butterflies and dragonflies abound. At one point it is necessary to negotiate a rock outcrop by balancing on the cast iron pipe but there are handholds and it presents no real problem. A little further on, as the path emerges from the trees, if one's balance is good, the stream can be crossed and re-crossed on this pipe in order to avoid a particularly marshy piece of ground.

Still following the stream reach the main road at the village of Edern. Here there is an inn, village store and craft & coffee shop. Turning left on the road cross the bridge and go up the hill where, just round the first bend, there is a kissing gate on the left. Keeping the hedge on the left proceed straight ahead to cross the farm access road and up the side of the next field to come out at the back of the golf clubhouse. Turning right down the approach road arrive back at the car park.

Walk 5 *10½ miles*
(plus 1½ miles to Aberdaron)

Tudweiliog - Traeth Penllech - Porthor - Anelog

OS Maps: 1:25 000 *Llŷn Peninsula West Explorer* 12
Start: Towyn Farm ½ mile north west of Tudweiliog village.
Access: Bus from Nefyn to village centre.
Parking: Towyn Farm
Grade: Moderate: Some short sharp ups & downs and paths not always well maintained.

(-) denotes Car walk
[-] denotes Point of interest

Walk Directions:
(A) Returning to the cliff top we follow round the bay on a definite path which, after ¼ mile or so drops down to what is a natural rock garden with waterfall and pool crossed by a plank. On the other side we pass through the few caravans at Porth Ysglaig and climb back up to the cliff top. After a further ½ mile we come to Porth Llydan with perhaps half a dozen fishing boats pulled up on the pebble beach. The tar covered hut set in the cliff top was apparently once used as a picnic shelter by the local landowner.

A little further round this low headland, dominated by the restored gable end of an old cottage we come to the little natural harbour of Porth Ysgadan.**[1]** Crossing the dirt track that serves as the road to the harbour we carry on along the cliff to Porth Gwylan,**(B)** another natural harbour. The next cove we drop down to is Porth Ychain, where the brick hut houses the rusting remains of a winch, and after climbing the steps on the

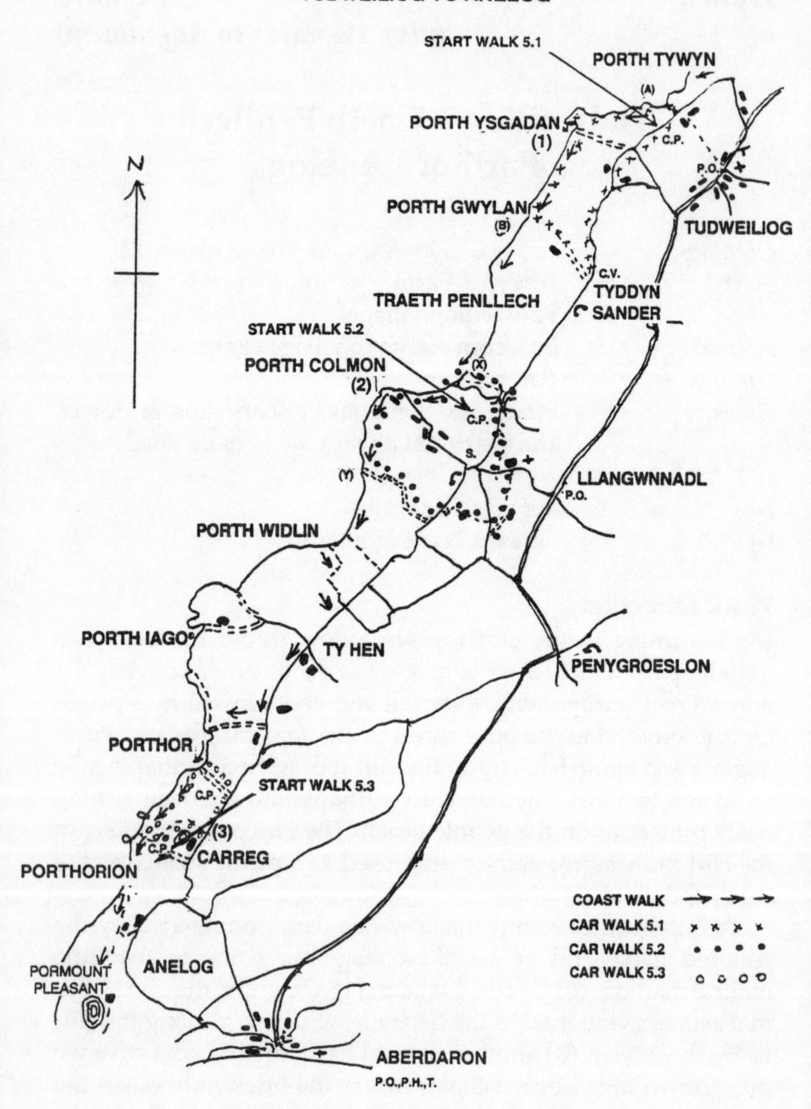
TUDWEILIOG TO ANELOG
START WALK 5.1
PORTH TYWYN
(A)
PORTH YSGADAN
(1)
C.P.
P.O.
PORTH GWYLAN
(B)
TUDWEILIOG
C.V.
TYDDYN
SANDER
TRAETH PENLLECH
START WALK 5.2
PORTH COLMON
(2)
(X)
C.P.
S.
(Y)
LLANGWNNADL
P.O.
PORTH WIDLIN
PORTH IAGO
TY HEN
PENYGROESLON
PORTHOR
START WALK 5.3
C.P.
(3)
C.P.
CARREG
PORTHORION
COAST WALK
CAR WALK 5.1
CAR WALK 5.2
CAR WALK 5.3
PORMOUNT
PLEASANT
ANELOG
ABERDARON
P.O.,P.H.,T.

far side bear off right to the cliff top. Following this round, over the next stile we drop down to another tiny cove. Going up the other side and around the edge of the field we pass through an opening in the fence and after 100 yards the path bears off right to continue along half way down the cliff. This leads to another stile and over a stream when, ignoring the one on the left we take the one in front to take the path, shared with livestock, again halfway down the cliff, leading to a small gate with another immediately in front which, with a scramble, drops down to the beach. This is Traeth Penllech,**(6)** which is in effect three bays separated, at high tide by rocky outcrops but becoming a mile long expanse of golden sand at low. At high tide it may be necessary to keep to the cliff top but along the shore is preferable.**(X)** At the far end of the second bay, after wading across a shallow river, which emerges, via a waterfall and narrow gorge, onto the beach we reach the third bay, but if due to the tide it is impossible to get round the rocks, then there are steps up the cliff to the path above, otherwise we continue to the far end where there is a slipway and boathouse. Going through the gate and up the steps we find that some thoughtful person has placed a welcome seat at the top which commands a magnificent view back along the bay. ¼ mile further on we drop down to the fishing cove of Porth Colmon.**[2]**

Crossing the cove pick up the cliff path through a kissing gate to the right of the stone house and up some steps. Here we have a wide grassy headland above a rocky shore with numerous secluded coves and a brilliantly clear sea.**(Y)** Following on along the path we cross a number of gullies which can become boggy; one has a wooden bridge another a plank but the remainder have to be negotiated as best one can – generally speaking it is easier to cross downstream. After just under 2 miles we come to a shallow gully and, ignoring the stile on the left, cross the plank and stile in front to turn right along the cliff where the secluded bay of Porth Widlin comes into sight.

The cliff path peters out at this point, since the local farmers have not allowed it to be carried on round the coast and we have to move inland onto the public roads before rejoining the path some 3 miles further on. This is a great pity since the coastline round Penrhyn Mawr headland is some of the finest. One particular beach on this section is open to the public, for a small payment, namely Porth Iago, **(7)** a narrow sandy cove popular with visitors, but this involves the walker with a round detour of 1¾ mile. This is all the more the pity since it is less than a mile to the N.T. land at Porth y Wrach, to where we are heading.

However not wishing to incur the wrath of the farmers we must dutifully head inland and looking for a pair of gateposts (no gate) in the hollow on the left pass through to the gate in front and then bearing left make for the gate into the next field. Then following the cart track across this field come out over a stile onto a lane and turn right. There is hardly any traffic on this lane and in just over ½ mile we turn right at the T-junction and, ignoring the road on the right, signposted to Porth lago, carry on for another ¾ mile looking for a footpath sign and kissing gate on the right – just after the new barn on the left and before the old one on the right. This leads, down a grass farm lane, to **(8)** Porthor (*Whistling Sands* – so called because they screech rather than whistle when walked on, due apparently to the rounded quartz crystals). This another magnificent beach between rocky headlands, popular with holiday makers, but never crowded and one of the few beaches to have a cafe and shop.

Here again dogs are not allowed so they and their owners will have to carry on along the road for a further mile until, just before a wood, there is a gate on the right onto N.T. Mynydd Carreg. Going round the base of the hill a kissing gate on the right gives onto a path back to the cliff top.**[3]**

Others who have crossed the sands pass in front c the cafe to pick up a path along the rocks and over a footbridge to steps up the cliff where a wide path makes for a pleasant stroll overlooking the wonderful coastal scenery. (There is an alternative path along the foot of the cliff but this can be treacherous after rain). Looking ahead, the white cottage just below the top of the distant hill in front, is the point for which we are making. Continuing along the cliff path for a little way it turns inland but down below, at Porthorion, will be seen a wooden bridge and stile to which there is an easy scramble down the grass slope. Climbing the hill in front we carry on the narrow path with the field fence on our left to a stile over a non-existent fence. We are now on open moorland where the purple heather and yellow gorse make a dazzling show. It is difficult to tell the paths from the sheep tracks, but carrying on upwards another stile is reached with a more distinct grass path beyond. On breasting the rise a wide vehicular track is seen on the next hill and we make for the hollow at the bottom of this.

As stated in the introduction accommodation can be a problem and apart from Carreg Plas mentioned earlier, it is unlikely that any will be found round here, certainly not for the next few miles of our route, apart from Aberdaron 1½ miles distant, which has two hotels, as well as B&B., cafes, shops, P.O. and toilets. The extra mileage is offset by booking in for two nights and being able to leave ones heavy belongings behind on the morrow. To get to Aberdaron then we leave the route here by taking the wide path on the left leading down to Anelog farm. After going through the farm gate and passed the duck pond on the right the path goes by the gable end of the building to the right front, through a gate and a short path comes out on the narrow lane. Carrying on straight ahead for 1¼ miles the road drops steeply down into the village. En route passing a Saints well at the cross-roads.

Points of Interest:

[1] On the right, just before passing through the gate there is a restored lime kiln. This was once a prolific herring harbour and though the herrings have long since gone is still a favourite place for fishermen off the rocks and for divers after lobsters these too are becoming harder to find. The roofless buildings in front once stored the goods, such as coal and lime, brought in by the small sailing vessels that served these remote country areas in the days before adequate roads.

[2] There is a village store and phone a mile up the road and ½ mile further the interesting pilgrims church of Llangwnnadl with a unique three naves and three altars. In 1901 the locals must have thought it was their birthday when the 'Stewart' carrying a cargo of whisky was wrecked hereabouts.

[3] The quarry at the base of the hill is where Jasper(the semi precious stone) was mined in the 18th and 19th centuries. The circular building on top of Mynydd Carreg is just a lookout but with fine views. Carreg Plas on the other side of the hill, once the ancient house of Welsh chiefs is now an hotel and might be suitable for those requiring accommodation, since the alternative is probably a detour into Aberdaron. Where the path from Carreg comes in on the left is a good spot to view the two small grass covered islands, Dinas Bach to the right and Dinas Fawr to the left, both joined to the mainland at low tide. The former usually has a couple of fishing boats hauled up on the beach.

CAR WALKS

5.1

Description:	A beautiful sandy cove; interesting cliff walk with two natural harbours; returning via country lanes.
Distance:	3 miles.
Time:	1½ hours.
Going:	Easy but can be muddy on the cliff path section.
Facilities:	None.
Start:	Towyn (232 375)

(A) Approaching from the Nefyn direction on the B4417 take the road on the right immediately after the Tudweiliog village sign. Signposted 'Traeth' ¾ mile down this road there is a car park with honesty box in the field of Tywyn farm.

Crossing the road enter the field and follow the path across to the cliff top. Follow now the directions in the main walk for the next 1½ miles to point **(B)** at Porth Gwylan. Here, after passing through the first wooden kissing gate, another will be found in 150 yards on the left with a finger post where we leave the main route to return to the car.

Pass through the gate onto the farm lane and then through the yard to reach the road in ¼ mile. Turn left on the road and where it makes a sharp righthand turn in 100 yards, bear left on the narrower road. Follow this lane round through Tyddyn Isaf farm and at the junction where a rough lane comes in on the left, turn right and almost immediately left at the next junction. The car park is ½ mile down this road.

5.2

Description:	A magnificent mile long beach; fine headland walk and return via fields and lanes passed an old pilgrim's church.
Distance:	4 miles.
Time:	2½ hours.
Going:	Moderate on the coastal section; rough inland – boots essential.
Facilities:	None.
Start:	Penllech (205 342)

Turning left out of the car park at Tywyn follow this minor road back over the route just walked. After passing through Tyddyn Isaf farm bear right at the next junction and keep straight on for 2 miles to where the road drops sharply down to a bridge over a stream. The free car park is on the right immediately over the bridge.

Leaving the car, recross the bridge and find a footpath immediately on the left which, after passing through two fields leads down to Traeth Penllech. Here we join the main walk **(X)** and follow those directions until a mile after leaving Porth Colmon come to the first steepish gully.**(Y)** Here the main route crosses over a stile in the bottom but we keep to the high side and follow it inland to a stile after which turn immediately left into a narrow sunken, very wet and overgrown lane. Over another stile and bearing right follow this lane, now becoming wider, passed ruined farm buildings on the right; over another stile with deserted farm on the right to finally emerge on the road about twenty minutes after leaving the coast.

Turn left on the road and, in ¼ mile just passed a corrugated iron shed, turn right at the footpath sign and immediately left through a narrow metal gate onto a raised, narrow, hedge lined path. The path becomes severely overgrown at the far end but press on and look for a small wooden gate which leads down to the field on the right. Cross to the white cottage and the path actually goes through two gates in the back yard. Cross the stream and go through the gate in front into a field. Go straight across to a stile and keeping to the right of this very muddy field come out, over a stile, onto a road. Turn right and 50 yards up the road turn left down the farm lane to Ty'n Rhos. Passing straight through the farmyard go through the gate in front and keeping to the hedge on the right take the left of the two gates across the field. Again keeping the hedge on the right find a well hidden wooden stile in the corner. Mid way along the far side of this next field is another well hidden stile leading into a rough field. Now keeping the hedge on the left drop down to a stile in the corner out onto a road.

The pretty old pilgrim's church of Llangwnnadl set in the wooded valley just 50 yards to the right is well worth a quick visit. However, turning left after emerging on the road there is a footpath on the right by the old village school some 50 yards away. Through the kissing gate in the school grounds bear half left up to a stile in the far corner. Keeping to the top of this very rough field and without any distinct path through the bracken, gorse and brambles, find a very well hidden stile in the far top corner which leads onto a proper field. Bear left to a stile across the field out onto the road. Turning right the car park is ½ mile down the road.

We cannot resist adding a short third walk to this section because of its scenic value.

5.3

Description:	A beach with whistling sands; a fine cliff top walk and a chance to find a semi-precious stone.
Distance:	2 miles.
Time:	1 hour.
Going:	Easy.
Facilities:	Café and toilets on beach. Picnic site at car park.
Start:	Mynydd Carreg (163 289)

Drive right out of the car park at Penllech; after ¾ mile turn right at the cross roads and then left by the phone box. After 2¼ miles by the farm Ty-hen turn right and bear left. In ½ mile at the next farm buildings (Methlem) turn right and in ¾ mile pass the entrance to Porthor **(8)** but carry on a little further beyond the wood in front. Just passed the farm at Plas Carreg turn right up the unmade lane alongside the farm buildings to a small N.T. car park and picnic site.

Go through the kissing gate in front and straight across the field which drops down to another gate and a path to the cliff top. However just before this gate a low waymarker shows a path going off to the right round the foot of the hill. This path emerges back on the road, passing on the way a quarry where at one time the semi-precious stone jasper was mined. Turn left down the road and left again down the rough access road to Whistling Sands. (Dogs are not allowed on this beach during the season.)

The dry sand on this beautiful bay emits a whistle when walked on, hence its name. There is a café at the foot of the approach incline in front of which there is a path over the rocks, across a foot bridge and up steps to the cliff top. There are magnificent views of the coastline with the two large offshore rocks of Dinas Bach and Dinas Fawr down below. The former has a tiny cove with a couple of boats drawn up on the beach. ¾ mile along the cliff top there is a well made (N.T.) kissing gate on the left which leads back up through the fields to the car park. The more energetic might wish to climb up to the lookout on top of Mynydd Carreg for fantastic views.

Walk 6 *7½ miles*
(plus 1½ miles from Aberdaron)

Anelog - Uwchmynydd - Mynydd Mawr - Pen y Cil - Port Meudwy - Aberdaron

OS Maps:	1:25 000 *Llŷn Peninsula West Explorer* 12
Start:	Anelog Farm 1½ miles from Aberdaron.
Access:	No bus routes.
Parking:	With difficulty on roadside.
Grade:	Rough: Some short sharp ups & downs and paths not always well maintained, rough underfoot with paths & stiles overgrown.

(-)	denotes Car walk
[-]	denotes Point of interest

Walk directions:
From the Aberdaron turnoff in the hollow at Anelog go straight ahead up the broad track in front. Half way up the hill ignore the track that goes off left keeping to the right of the fenced off area. Again keeping to the wider path ignore the next on the left and at the brow of the hill another fenced off experimental area. Now follow the broad track up to and round behind the white cottage Mount Pleasant in front. Ignore the narrow path that goes off to the right which leads to a spring and up onto Mynydd Anelog, and follow the more prominent path round the southerly shoulder of the mountain. There are good views here of the bottom end of the peninsula.

After passing above a near derelict cottage the path begins to descend, passing through a small gate, and coming to an unoccupied cottage with black shed down on the right. In front of this cottage as the main path widens, bends to the left and starts to rise slightly, there is an overgrown sunken path

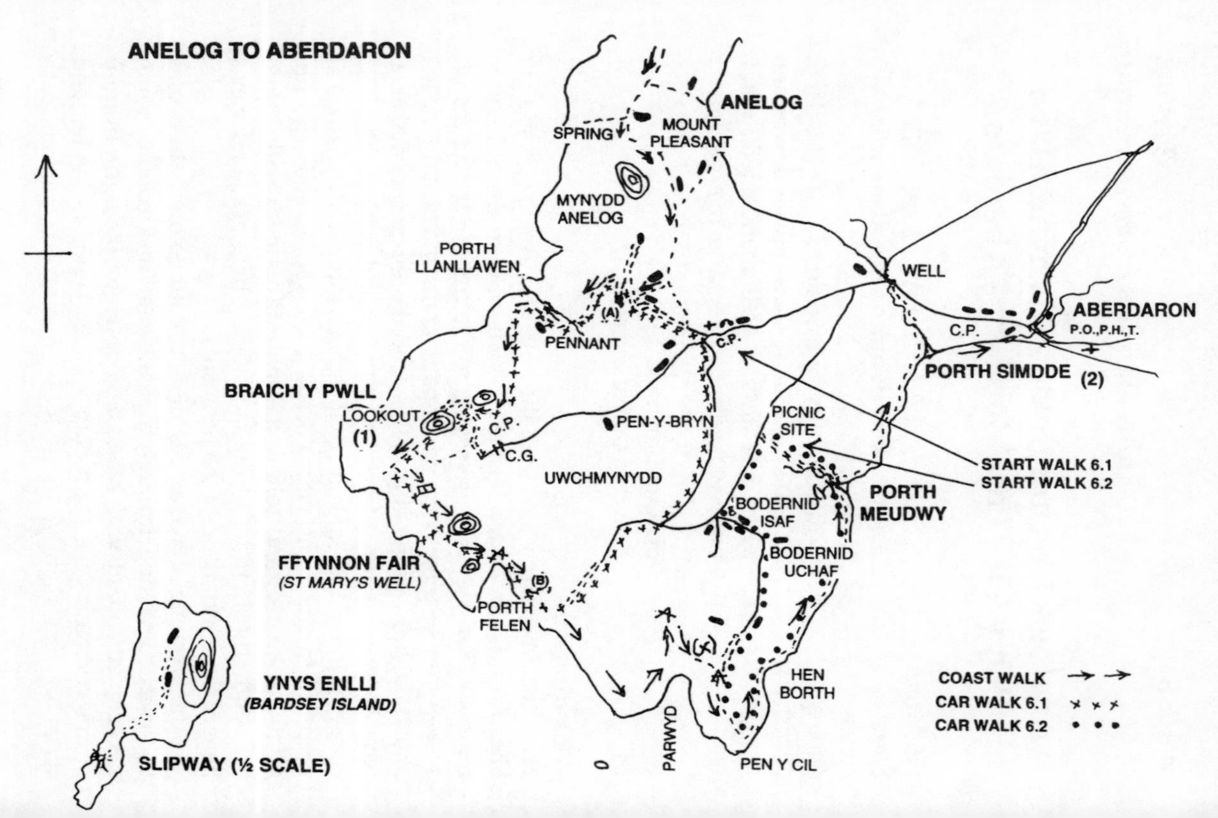
ANELOG TO ABERDARON
ANELOG
SPRING
MOUNT
PLEASANT
MYNYDD
ANELOG
PORTH
LLANLLAWEN
(A)
PENNANT
WELL
ABERDARON
P.O.,P.H.,T.
C.P.
C.P.
PORTH SIMDDE
(2)
BRAICH Y PWLL
LOOKOUT
(1)
C.P.
C.G.
PEN-Y-BRYN
PICNIC
SITE
START WALK 6.1
START WALK 6.2
UWCHMYNYDD
PORTH
MEUDWY
BODERNID
ISAF
BODERNID
UCHAF
FFYNNON FAIR
(ST MARY'S WELL)
(B)
PORTH
FELEN
YNYS ENLLI
(BARDSEY ISLAND)
SLIPWAY (½ SCALE)
PARWYD
PEN Y CIL
HEN
BORTH
COAST WALK
CAR WALK 6.1
CAR WALK 6.2

straight ahead which, after a few yards leads to a stile and across a field with a large black barn to the left to drop onto a dirt road.**(A)** There are waymarkers bearing a Celtic cross in this area, marking the route of the pilgrims as they neared the end of their journey. Turning right in about 20 yards the road divides, one branch turning back on itself to a farm, the other bearing right to two more farms, but we take the waymarked grass track in front through a gate down a very short grass lane into a field. Following round the left-hand side of the field making for a gap into the next field with another white cottage across the valley in front. Heading towards this we come to a stile in the far left corner with a bracken covered path down to a stream and up to the garden gate of the cottage named Pennant. A Celtic cross marker points right and we follow the fence along until progress is barred by a fence after 250 yards. There is a fine view, over Porth Llanllawen, of the sheer cliffs. This is mainly N.T. land round here. There seems to be a stile missing but it is fairly easy to negotiate the fence on the left and keeping the fence on the left another in the top left corner out onto the open ground beyond. In the absence of a specific path follow the line of the fence on the left steeply uphill. Where the fence veers off left do likewise but keep climbing to a rocky knoll and rounding the shoulder of the main hill drop down to a green wall in the depression. Follow this for a few paces and where it goes off left keep straight ahead up the hill to emerge suddenly onto a narrow concrete road. This takes us up to the now abandoned coastguard lookout on top of Mynydd Mawr.**[1]**

We descend from the summit by a concrete footpath and steps, just to the left of the coastguard buildings, down to the first level, with the remains of former service huts, and then to the next level where there is a mine adit, and follow the grass path to the left which takes us round the hillside where we can see down in front the outline of a former building. At one time it was thought that this was the remains of a chapel but now thought more likely to be that of a farm. We cross this field to a gully leading down to the sea at the bottom of which is Ffynnon

Fair (*St Mary's well*). It is covered at high water but the fresh water bubbles through – it is not easy to find. Returning now up the gully there are, on the right, two small fenced enclosures where the N.T. are carrying out plant research, but just before the second we take the track that leads up the next hill Mynydd Gwyddel. Following one of the many sheep tracks either round the shoulder or over the top we make, in a south easterly direction for a stile in the corner down below at the head of the narrow inlet Porth Felen. Keeping to the seaward side of this field another stile takes us out onto the open headlands.**(B)**

From here round to Aberdaron is what must be one of the most dramatic cliff walks but extra care must be taken since for most of the way the path, narrow and unfenced, runs along the edge of sheer drops.

There is no clear path through this N.T. area but after 400 yards there is a fence with a stile, in the middle and continuing round this open headland we come to the vertical cliffs of Parwyc where we have to turn up to a fence. 50 yards to the left is a stile. Keeping the next field boundary on our left and after passing through a gate another stile on the right with a N.T. sign announcing that this is Pen y Cil.**(X)** a S.S.S.I. Going up to the cairn we get a magnificent view of the 1½ mile Aberdaron Bay with its two islands Ynys Gwylan Fawr and Bach (noted for their colonies of puffins) and back to Ynys Enlli. From here down to the cliff path is a little tricky since there is no recognisable path, but proceeding in a S.E. direction keeping as far as possible to the tracts of grass rather than the gorse and heather hit the path on the cliff edge. There is a path shown on the O.S. which goes north but higher up the hillside and which leads inland. As a guide, from the top we can look down on the stone wall of an abandoned enclosure – our path is to the seaward side of this.

From here on the path is fairly obvious since it hugs the cliff edge and again we repeat our warning to take care especially if it is muddy under foot. In ½ mile the remains of a tiny harbour can be seen below at Porth y Pistyll, the only access to which seems to be from the sea, but a little further on there is a small quarry which presumably used the harbour. Ignoring the stile on the left we keep to the face of the quarry rather than trying to go over the top and after a little scramble regain the more clear path. In a further ½ mile we come to the small fishing cove of Porth Meudwy, from whence the pilgrims set sail on the usually rough crossing to Ynys Enlli. Just before dropping down to the cove, ignoring the stile on the left, we take the one in front and follow the steep winding path to the bottom.**(Y)** Crossing the stream and – wending our way through the lobster pots and fishing boats we climb the steps on the other side, where, after passing through two kissing gates we come out on the open headland again. Another ½ mile brings us to Porth Simdde where we branch off the main path onto the one leading down to the stumps of the old wooden jetty. From here it is but a 200 yard walk into the village of Aberdaron **(9)**.

People with dogs should carry on along the main path, over a footbridge and up the valley where, after 500 yards we come out on the road. Turning right the village is reached ½ mile downhill, entered over a medieval hump backed bridge.**[2]**

With a winter population of less than 1,000 there are two hotels, B&B, cafes, P.O., toilets and the village is on a bus route.

Points of interest:

[1] This is Braich y Pwll, from where the views are spectacular from Anglesey in the north to the Preseli hills in Pembrokeshire (where some of the stones of Stonehenge came from) in the south and in front, 2 miles across the notoriously treacherous Sound, Ynys Enlli (Bardsey Island). The island is roughly 1 mile long by ½ mile, rising to a height of 547 feet. The western side and southern end are flat and there were once six farms. The monastery was founded by St. Cadfan in the 5th.C. but the only remains to be seen today are those of the 13th.C. Augustinian St. Mary's Abbey where the 20,000 saints are said to be buried along with Lord Newborough in 1888. The island is now a bird and field observatory noted for Manx sheerwaters and apart from the warden is uninhabited, though it is possible to visit if enquiries are made in Aberdaron. The lighthouse was established in 1821 and is now fully automatic. Cardigan Bay to the south is the home of bottle nose dolphins as well as porpoises and even the odd small whale. Note too the ancient long narrow field patterns to the south.

For more information: *Tomos the Islandman,* J. Jones, £4, (*Gwasg Carreg Gwalch*), well illustrated by local artist, Kim Atkinson.)

Before leaving the summit look over the wall, just to the right of the lookout, at the sheer drop of 500 feet to the sea. During both world wars the point was a defended lookout, hence the concrete road up. A number of ships were sunk off Ynys Enlli including six torpedoed in five days in February 1917; others were bombed during WW2.

[2] Aberdaron's main claim to fame is its connection with the pilgrims. The Cegin Fawr, where waiting pilgrims fed now feeds the holiday makers. The church, whose graveyard has had to be protected from the encroaching sea, dedicated to St Hywyn, dates back to the 12th.C. Inside are two inscribed burial stones dating from the 6th.C. The old post office was designed by Clough Williams Ellis of Portmeirion fame. The village's most famous character was probably Dic Aberdaron (Richard Robert Jones) who, in the late 18th.C., was a self taught linguist – some say he could speak 15 languages others 35!. He compiled a Welsh, Greek and Hebrew dictionary which can be seen in St Asaph Cathedral where he is buried. In 1405 the Tripartite Indenture was signed here whereby Wales would be independent under Owain Glyndŵr, North England under the Percys and the south under the Mortimers – a plan ruined by Henry IV.

CAR WALKS:

6.1

Description:	Some of the finest coastal scenery with views across to Ynys Enlli; return along a quiet country lane.
Distance:	4 miles.
Time:	2½ hours.
Going:	Rough.
Facilities:	None except in Aberdaron.
Start:	Uwchmynydd (155 264)

From Aberdaron take the minor road heading west, up the steep hill out of the village. In just over ½ mile turn left at the staggered crossroads. Keep straight ahead for ¾ mile, passed a chapel on the left and immediately after rounding a steep bend with a corrugated building on the right, there is a parking place on the right in front of the next chapel by the phone box.

A few yards west of the phone box take the cul-de-sac lane on the right. Ignoring the signed footpath that shortly goes up to the right keep straight ahead through a farm gate into an open field. Follow the farm lane round passed the farm house and rounding a bend the lane divides. Here is where we join the main walk **(A)** and take the grass track in front.

Keep to the main walk directions right round the headland to point **(B)** just beyond Porth Felen. Here keep to the top side of the open ground where just, before the fence in front there are two gates on the left, the one on the right leads onto a green lane. Follow this up, passed two cottages on the left where it becomes tarmac. Continue straight ahead and in 500 yards take the first road on the left. (not the rough lane before the farm.) ¾ mile down this road turn right at the T-junction and the car should be in front.

6.2

Description:	A quiet country lane followed by some magnificent cliff scenery and a tiny fishing cove.
Distance:	3 miles.
Time:	1¾ hours.
Going:	Moderate.
Facilities:	None except in Aberdaron. Picnic site at start.
Start:	N.T. Cwrt (159 259)

From Uwchmynydd return towards Aberdaron and, after ½ mile, take the first road on the right. After ½ mile look out for a N.T. sign and track on the left leading down to Porth Meudwy. There is a picnic site and car park just off the road.

Walk along the road for a further ½ mile to a cluster of buildings and post box. This is Bodermid Isaf and turn left here to pass the next farm Bodermid Uchaf. This road ends in a farm gate leading into an open field with a farm track across. Keep straight ahead ignoring the track going off to the right, pass through another gateway and head across the field to the fence and stile on the skyline. Beware the fence is electrified!

Here join point **(X)** on the main walk and proceed up to Pen y Cil. Follow the directions round the coastal path and drop down to the beach at Porth Meudwy **(Y)**. Follow the track back up the valley to the car park.

Walk 7 ***11 miles***

Aberdaron - Porth Cadlan - Porth Ysgo - Mynydd Penarfynydd - Rhiw - Porth Neigwl - Llanengan

OS Maps:	1:25 000 *Llŷn Peninsula West Explorer* 12
Start:	Aberdaron car park.
Access:	Infrequent bus service from Pwllheli.
Parking:	Main car park
Grade:	Moderate: Some short sharp ups & downs and paths not always well maintained.

(-)	denotes Car walk
[-]	denotes Point of interest

Walk directions:

If the tide is not too high we can walk along the sands until, after ½ mile there is a cleft in the cliff where a rough path leads up to a field where the gate opposite opens onto a farm lane and shortly comes out on the road. If the tide is high then we take the steep road by the church and after ¾ mile meet the farm lane coming in on the right. This is another headland on which there is no public footpath and we must perforce keep to the road for the next ¾ mile to a row of cottages on the left opposite which is an easily missed stile – under the power cables which cross the road at this point. Going up the field we come to another stile and bearing left down an old farm lane pass in front of the farmhouse and through the gate in front. Keeping to the side of the field and over a stile in the corner we go into the left one of the two fields in front which takes us down to the farm Cadlan Uchaf, which we pass on our right coming out onto the farm lane. A quick left and a right leads to

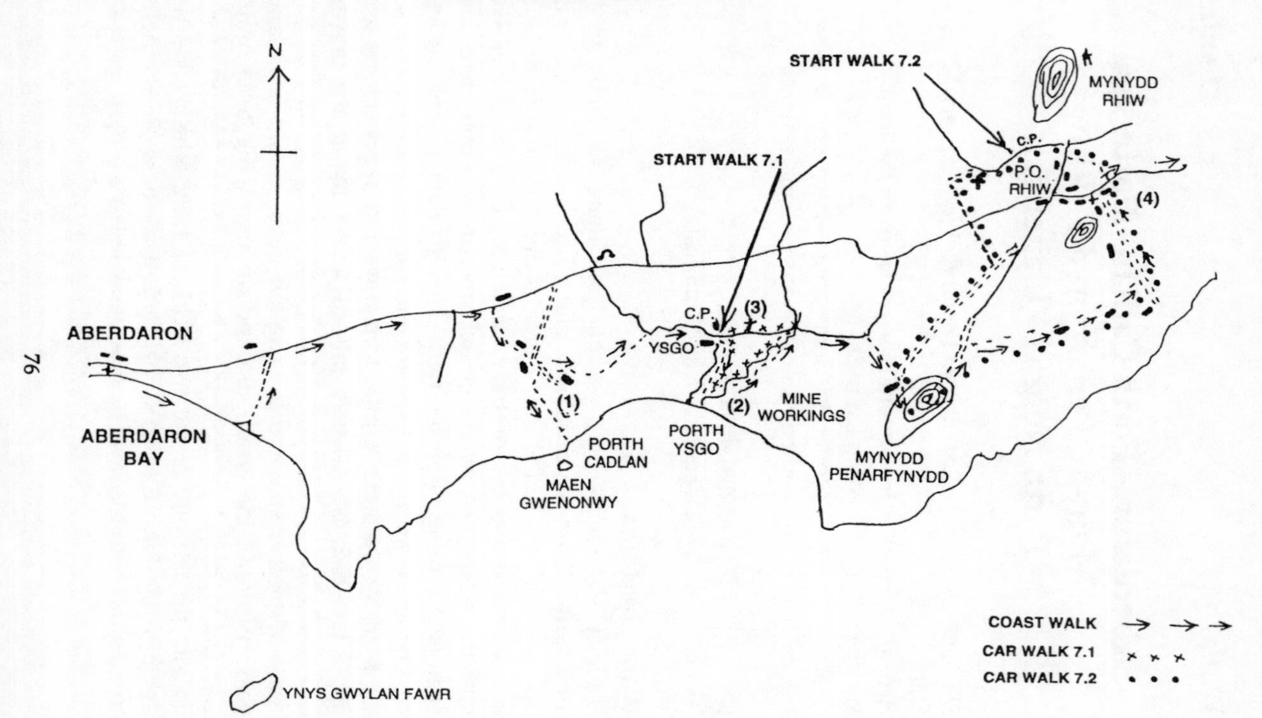
ABERDARON TO RHIW
N
START WALK 7.2
MYNYDD RHIW
C.P.
P.O.
RHIW
(4)
START WALK 7.1
C.P.
(3)
YSGO
ABERDARON
ABERDARON BAY
(1)
(2)
MINE WORKINGS
PORTH YSGO
PORTH CADLAN
MAEN GWENONWY
MYNYDD PENARFYNYDD
COAST WALK
CAR WALK 7.1
CAR WALK 7.2
YNYS GWYLAN FAWR
YNYS GWYLAN BACH

the next farm, Cadlan Isaf. The gate across the lane is usually locked but there is a stile.**[1]**

Returning now to the farm lane we do not go into the yard but look for a stile in the left corner behind the farm buildings. Keeping to the right of this field; over a stile; to the left of the next; through a gate; bearing left and two more stiles bring us out onto a lane. Turning right we quickly pass a duck pond and the deserted Ysgo farmhouse on the left and take the signposted footpath on the right by the farm buildings. This leads, through a kissing gate, onto N.T. land of Porth Ysgo. **(10)** **(A)** The path goes down the left-hand side of the valley where, at the bottom, wooden steps descend to this small sandy bay. Returning to the path we carry on round the hillside into the next valley Nant y Gadwen.

Ahead will be seen the spoil heaps of the manganese mines which operated in this area from the mid 19th.C. until 1946.**[2]** The path carries on up the valley through a kissing gate. The main mine shaft is up on the right just before the path crosses a stone footbridge, but take care, it is unfenced. The path shortly comes out on a lane **(B)** where we turn right.**[3]**

¼ mile along the lane, where it bears left, there is, on the right, a footpath sign, gate and stile. We follow the path on the left of the first field, crossing to the right of the next and come out at the farm Penarfynydd.**(X)** Crossing the yard and through a gate behind the house we come onto the open hillside. This is Mynydd Penarfynydd a S.S.S.I. and, turning right and climbing diagonally to the top it is worth spending a little time exploring and admiring the magnificent views, before making for the trig. point.

(Those who don't wish to climb can turn left and follow the path round the base of the hill to the stile.)

Heading down the grass spur from the trig. point towards the stile at the bottom, passed a small sewage plant come to a grass lane where, 50 yards after passing through a gate go over a stile on the right onto the open headland with a marvellous display of gorse and heather. This is Mynydd y Graig and

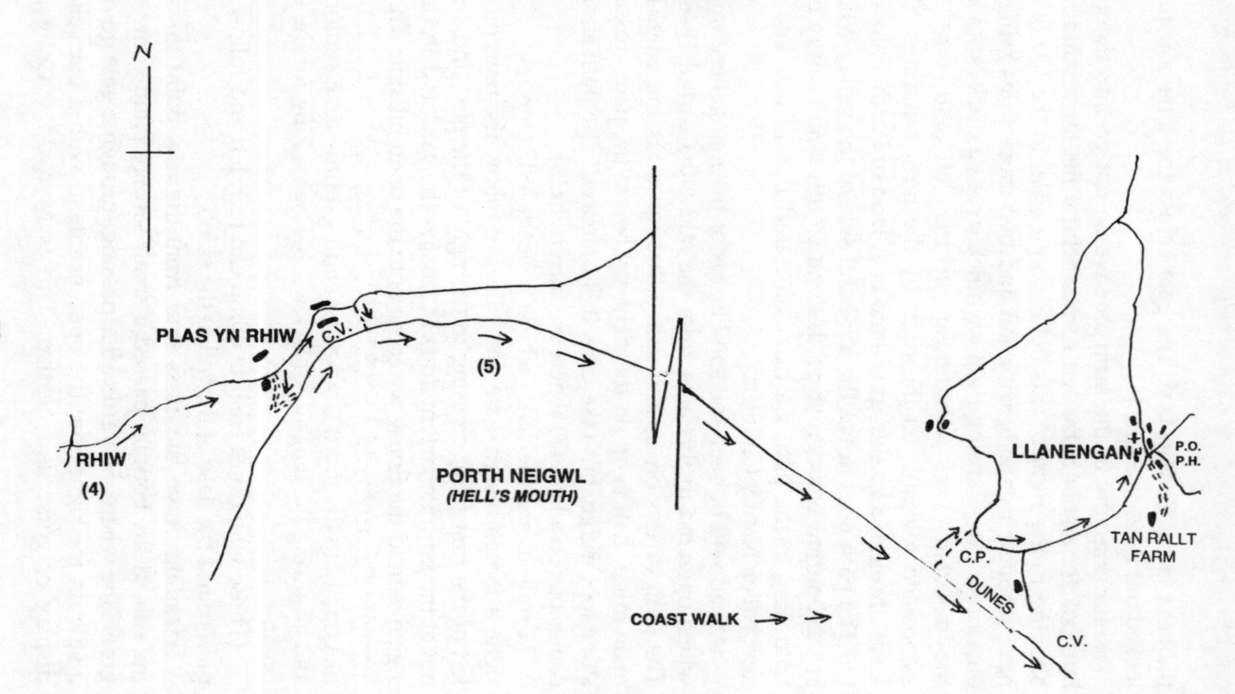
RHIW TO LLANENGAN
N
PLAS YN RHIW
C.V.
(5)
RHIW
(4)
PORTH NEIGWL
(HELL'S MOUTH)
LLANENGAN
P.O.
P.H.
TAN RALLT
FARM
C.P.
DUNES
COAST WALK
C.V.

following the obvious path round the headland through the bracken it drops slightly and then starts to rise to meet a walled enclosure. Keeping to the upper side head for the gable end of the cottage in front. Passing behind the cottage the path rises fairly steeply to a rock outcrop. It then drops down to meet a wider track by a gate. Turn left through the gate, passed a row of three cottages, the last called Bay View, and then another gate before going by a cluster of cottages to come out on the main road in Rhiw.**(Y)** The P.O./ shop is 300 yards to the left, but turn right down the hill with the panorama of Porth Neigwl (Hell's Mouth) (11) in front.**[4]** Proceeding on the road down the hill we can now see the full extent of Porth Neigwl Bay.**[5]**

At the bottom of the hill just after the entrance to Plas yn Rhiw, a small manor house given to the N.T. in 1952 by the Keating sisters, we go in front of the small barn on the right where a track signed 'Unsuitable for cars' winds down to a ruined cottage on the beach with several small fishing boats and huts. From here it is a rather rough 200 yards over boulders to the sandy beach. Alternatively we can continue down the road where there is a stile 200 yards passed Treheli farm and caravan site.

Walking in sand can be tiring but about halfway along the shore it is reasonably easy to gain access to the dunes where the going is better, but be careful, the cliffs are unstable and are being eroded at the rate of 1 ft/year. Care should also be taken when swimming for there are currents. During WW2 there was an airfield on the flat hinterland with a gunnery and bombing range out to sea. Two thirds of the way along the shore we must leave it to get to Llanengan for those requiring accommodation, whilst campers can carry on if they wish. The path from the beach is obvious and leads to the road at the car park. Turning right an easy ¾ mile takes us into the village. Apart from the Sun Inn there is a fine church used by the pilgrims with bells supposedly taken from the Abbey on Ynys Enlli, and a P.O/shop.

Points of interest:

[1] A recent study has suggested, with ample evidence to link him to the area, that this is the site of the last battle fought by King Arthur and that after being wounded he was taken by boat from Porth Cadlan to Ynys Enlli. A short diversion here might be of interest since it traverses the alleged fields of battle. In this case we head down to, and across, the small stream in the hollow, turning left to follow it to a stile that leads onto the headland. Down below is a large grass covered rock, Maen Gwenonwy, which is an island at high tide but accessible at low, though it is doubtful if the effort is worthwhile.

For more information: *Walks on the Llŷn Peninsula, Part 1 South and West*, Burras/Stiff, £4.50, (Gwasg Carreg Gwalch.)

[2] The heyday of the mines was during the two world wars. This mine produced over 45,000 tons of ore during its lifetime. A pier was built at Porth Alwm in 1902 at a cost of £182, with an incline down to take the ore from this mine and others further inland. The pier has gone but the line of the incline and associated buildings, which included a weighbridge, can still be seen.

[3] There is an interesting little church 200 yards back along the lane.

[4] The whole of this area abounds with archaeological remains. The field on our right as we came up the hill contains traces of hut circles, enclosures, and platform houses; the craggy summit on the left has been a hill fort; Mynydd Rhiw ahead has a Neolithic stone axe factory on its northern slope, a burial chamber down on the eastern side and remains of a homestead to the south. Of a much later date are the remains of manganese mines at the foot of the mountain. Over 60,000 tons of ore were produced during WW2, taken by an aerial ropeway to a pier at the foot of the hill we have just come up. Of a still later date, the radar station on the mountain belongs to the M.O.D. in connection with their activities further down Cardigan Bay.

[5] Its four mile stretch of sand looks inviting but its English name suggests otherwise. Many a ship has come to grief on these shores. In 1898, the good ship *Twelve Apostles* was blown ashore fortunately with no loss of life but the captain's message to Lloyds read *'Twelve apostles making water in Hell's Mouth'*. Others were not so lucky; in 1629 a French vessel carrying members of the aristocracy, lured by the false light of the wreckers, hit the rocks and it is said that the locals attacked the survivors with such ferocity killing many and cutting off their fingers for their rings. Thereafter seafarers had a dread of being stranded on these shores. Apart from wreckers on land there were pirate ships at sea in the l7th.C., and, surprisingly, Arab traders, who in one raid on Holyhead, captured over 100 persons for the white slave markets of northern Africa.

CAR WALKS:

7.1

Description:	Short but worthwhile walk to a lovely cove; reminders of the areas industrial past; a tiny pilgrims church.
Distance:	1 mile.
Time:	¾ hour.
Going:	Moderate but steep steps down to the actual beach.
Facilities:	None.
Start:	Ysgo (207 268)

Taking the steep road passed the church out of Aberdaron in 2 miles take the narrow road on the right opposite the phone box. In ½ mile come to a duck pond and deserted Ysgo farm. Park off the road here.**(A)** Follow the main directions to visit the cove and back up to the road at **(B)**. Turn left to return to the car on the way passing the tiny church of St Maelrhys.

7.2

Description:	Gentle walk through lanes and fields to a short but fine coastal path. Extensive views in all directions.
Distance:	3 miles.
Time:	1½ hours.
Going:	Moderate.
Facilities:	Shop/P.O. in Rhiw.
Start:	Rhiw (225 281)

Approaching from Aberdaron turn left at the cross roads in the hamlet of Rhiw. (coming from the Abersoch direction turn right). Passed the P.O. and village hall follow the road round to the left and in 100 yards or so find a parking space on the grass verge. (Please don't block the gateways).

Carry on walking down the hill with more remains of the manganese mines in on the right and with views ahead to Aberdaron and Ynys Enlli. Just after the chapel, where the road bears right, go straight ahead down the Green Lane, turning left at the bottom. Through the metal gate continue to the road at Tyddyn Meirion. (A donkey sometimes lives on this part of the land but he seems friendly enough.)

Cross the road to a stile almost directly in front and keep straight on through three fields towards a derelict farm. Turn left down what, in theory, should be the old farm access lane – in practice this has been blocked off so take to the edge of the field to join the lane a little further on. Negotiate a gate tied with rope and then bear right up to a made-up farm drive and out through the gate onto the tarmac road at a Y-junction.

Take the lane to the right and in ½ mile come to the N.T. farm of Penarfynydd. Join here the main walk **(X)** and cross the farmyard to the access gate.

Having followed the main route round the coast as far as Rhiw turn right on the main road and in a few yards leave the route **(Y)** through a waymarked kissing gate on the left. Cross the field to the prominent stile opposite and then follow the righthand field boundary round to come out on a rough lane, turn left to join the road. Turn right and follow the road round to the left to find the car just in front.

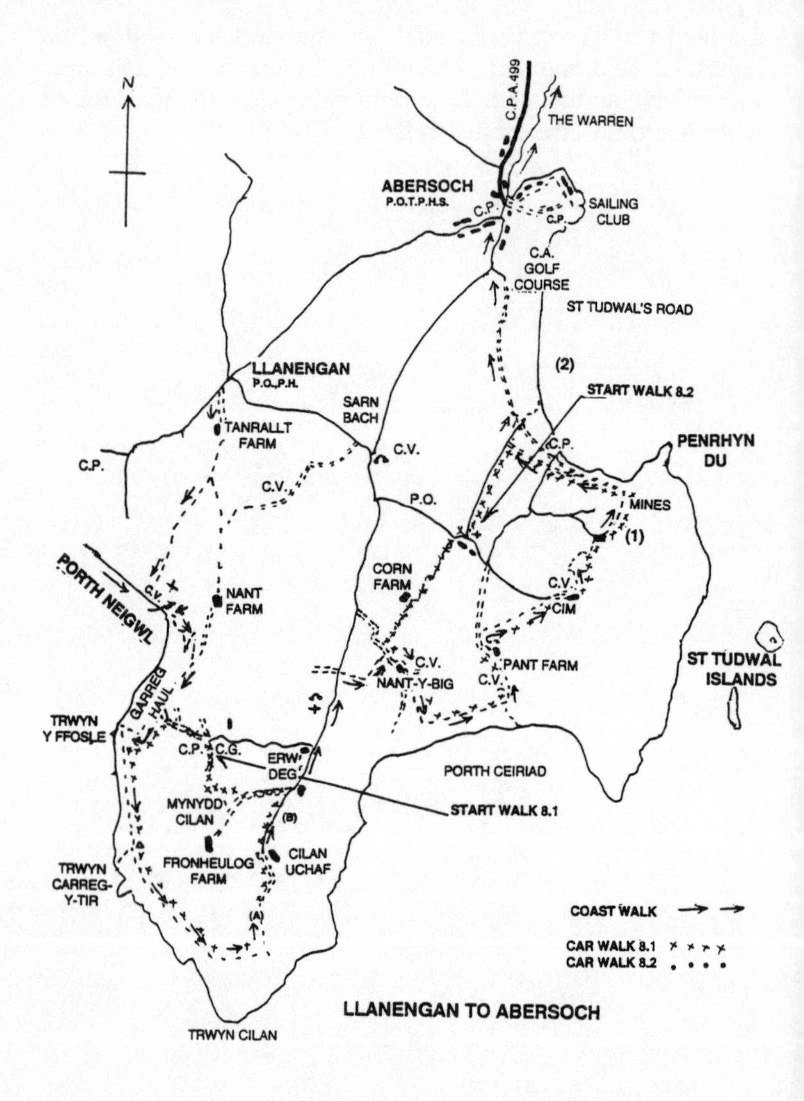

LLANENGAN TO ABERSOCH

Walk 8 *9 miles*

Llanengan - Mynydd Cilan - Porth Ceiriad - Abersoch

OS Maps:	1:25 000 *Llŷn Peninsula West Explorer* 12
Start:	Llanengan Sun Inn.
Access:	Infrequent bus service from Pwllheli.
Parking:	Difficult in village. Good car park ½ mile from village, sign posted Porth Neigwl (*Hells Mouth*)
Grade:	Moderate: Some short sharp ups & downs and paths not always well maintained.

(-)	denotes Car walk
[-]	denotes Point of interest

Walk directions:

Taking the path to the left of the Sun Inn, passed the spoil heap of the old lead and zinc mine with its smelting chimney above, we come to Tan Rallt farm. Shortly after this the path divides, the one to the right, which we take, leaves the bottom of the cliff and heads diagonally across two fields to come out on the dunes in the corner of Porth Neigwl (*Hell's Mouth Bay*). To the left is a small flat field just above the beach, with usually two or three caravans and in the far, seaward corner a stile. Just over this, in the grass, is the outline of what used to be a large concrete arrow pointing to the bombing target in the bay. Keeping to the right of this field to start with and then striking up half right in the direction of a ruined cottage on the skyline we pass to the right of this to reach a stile in the corner. At the far side of the field in front we come on a farm track and turning right through a gate pass in front of the cottages on the right. **(A)**

This open ground, part N.T. and part common land, is Trwyn Cilan a heathland S.S.S.I. with magnificent views all round and a colourful display of flora. Turning right round the end of the enclosure on the right and taking the broad path facing Porth Neigwl, keeping the radio mast on Rhiw mountain directly ahead, we turn left just before it starts to descend sharply and head towards the trig. point. Where the path meets the corner of a wall a steep gully leads down to Trwyn y Fossle (Fossil Point) which may be of interest to some who are prepared to scramble down and back up. Continuing now along the obvious path to the trig. point just after which there is a track leading down to the prominent hillock on the cliff edge, known as Trwyn Carreg y Tir, to which it is well worth diverting to view the interesting rock strata of the cliffs and traces of mining activity. Returning to the route follow the wide path round the open headland for perhaps ½ mile till it turns sharply left up to the brow of the hill. Take a last look back towards the end of the peninsula and in front to the two islands off Abersoch; St Tudwal's East, with remains of a priory and West with a lighthouse. Cross to a stile immediately in front and, keeping the wall on our right, come to another over which bear slightly left across the field making for the farm buildings which are approached by a short lane. This is Cilan Uchaf **(B)** and passing through the yard we come out on a metalled lane down which we continue for just under a mile. Looking over to the right, opposite a road coming in on the left, can be seen the remains of a coastal fort occupying a prominent position overlooking Porth Ceiriad.

Just after the chapel and phone box a lane comes in on the left, immediately opposite which are steps up to a stile. Keeping the hedge on our right we cross another stile and then, veering away from the hedge slightly, come to a well made stile across the field leading onto a small area of open heath. The rough track passed the fronts of the houses on the left brings us to a lane.**(X)** Turning right we pass a small caravan site and, where the lane turns into Nant y Big farm, we take the left of the two gates in the angle of the road turning immediately right to follow a bracken covered path down towards the sea. At the bottom it opens out into a wide flat area overlooking Porth Ceiriad.(12) This is another beautiful beach with a ½ mile stretch of sand and is well worth the effort of descending the steps at the far end. Another S.S.S.I. noted for choughs and auks.

Unfortunately the headland at the far side of the bay is private property with no official right of way, which is a shame since it contains some of the best rugged coastal scenery, and we are obliged to cut inland. At the far side of the open space a well defined track leads up the little valley to a caravan site where the path runs along the right-hand side onto the site approach road and Pant farm. 50 yards down the lane take the stile on the right by the cattle grid and then, keeping the hedge on our left, cross the next stile continuing diagonally half left towards a gap and another stile. Still keeping to the left of the fields, and heading towards the big white farmhouse come to a stile onto the approach road to Cim farm and caravan site. Turn right to pass in front of the house with the remains of a wellhead pump in the garden. Opposite is a kissing gate and following round the left of the field go through the farm gate into the next field on the left. Follow this field round towards a house in the far corner where a stile leads round the back of the house and edge of garden onto a lane. Bearing right onto what now becomes a rough road enter an area that was once a hive of industry.**[1]**

Continue down what has now become more of a river bed and turn left at the bottom along the edge of the cliff overlooking Abersoch beach **(13)** passing behind the houses with their access to the shore. This path was once the trackbed of a tramway carrying lead ore from another mine on the golf course to the old jetty. Shortly cross the minor road which leads to a car park and slipway giving access to the beach. (Dogs are allowed on this part of the shore as far as the beach huts). Continue to a T-junction **(Y)** and turn right down to the golf course with an old lead mine and a S.S.S.I. on the left. Follow the path across the course to the back of the club house and pick up the tarmac road which leads up to the main road where a right turn and a 200 yard walk brings you to the centre of the village.

Those who have elected to walk along the sand carry on to the far end leaving by the rather ugly beach chalets passed the cafe to the entrance of the car park behind. Turning immediately right takes us up to a higher car park behind the sailing club where a path will be found going round the headland behind the houses to drop down into the village by the harbour.[2] With a large summer population the village is well provided with hotels and restaurants as well as all the other facilities.

Points of interest:

[1] Lead mining has been carried on here from Roman times and particularly during the 17th.,18th., and 19th.C., finally being abandoned at the end of the latter. All that remains are a spoil heap on the left, the pump house on the right and a row of cottages, known as 'Cornish Row', after the tin miners who were brought in to work the mines. The main shafts are in private property to the right. The ore was taken down the path we are on to a jetty at the, now disused, lifeboat station.

[2] In contrast to Porth Neigwl, St Tudwal's Road was considered a safe anchorage, despite a fair number of vessels coming to grief over the years. At one time it was planned to build a breakwater out from Penrhyn Du to provide an even safer anchorage and to protect vessels loading ore, but with the closure of the mines and the decline of sailing ships the plan was not proceeded with. Nevertheless, Abersoch has become a very popular sailing harbour as witness the many yachts anchored off the sailing club in the season.

CAR WALKS:

8.1

Description:	A wide open headland with magnificent views and plenty of fresh air. Interesting rock formations.
Distance:	3 miles.
Time:	1½ hours.
Going:	Moderate.
Facilities:	None.
Start:	Mynydd Cilan (295 247)

Leave Abersoch on the road to Sarn Bach and in a mile go straight ahead at the cross roads in that hamlet. Continue for a mile to a chapel and phone box on the right. ¼ mile further on turn right by the bungalow Erw Deg. (actually this is the first proper road on the right after leaving Sarn Bach).Continue a further ¼ mile to a cattle grid that leads out onto open ground and park on the grass.

Walk straight ahead along the centre one of the three gravel tracks leading out from the cattle grid. Shortly where the track divides keep to the left and come up in front of the bungalow Garreg Haul. The main walk comes in from the right here **(A)**. Turn left to join it. Follow the main walk right round the headland to the farm Cilan Uchaf, leaving the yard by the tarmac road **(B)**. Continue as far as a dwelling on the right and turn left down the farm lane to Fronheulog opposite. Go down the lane, passed the back of the first farm to a cattle grid. Don't go over this but go through the gate to the right in front into a field. Keeping to the left of this field climb the gate at the far side back onto the common land. Turn right on the path and pick up a wider track which follows the edge of the common as far as a house and then swings left passed a pond and then curving right round a wet area. Keep heading in a north direction and shortly pick up a gravel track. Turn right on this and follow it back to the car.

8.2

Description:	A pleasant walk through fields to the popular beach of Porth Ceiriad and then the even more popular beach of Abersoch with passing reminders of the area's industrial past.
Distance:	3½ miles.
Time:	2 hours .
Going:	Moderate.
Facilities:	P.O./shop near start.
Start:	Bwlchtocyn (311 261)

If returning from Trwyn Cilan turn left down the road back to Sarn Bach but just over a mile take the road that goes steeply up to the right just before that hamlet. If coming from Abersoch it is the first road on the left after the cross roads in Sarn Bach, signposted to Bwlchtocyn. Proceed up the hill passed the P.O. to an estate of white painted houses on the right and a chapel on the left. There is parking space on the grass verge this side of the chapel.

Crossing the road walk back a few yards to find a kissing gate on the left at the start of the drive to a house. Go down the field alongside the white estate to another kissing gate at the bottom. Turn right and follow the hedge up to the far corner turning right into the next field and then left down the short farm lane to Corn farm. Keeping the farm buildings on the right leave the yard by another short lane and cross the next two fields, keeping the fence on the right to emerge onto a narrow tarmac road. Turn left and join the main walk which comes in from the right just before the small caravan site.**(X)**

Follow the directions for the main walk practically to Abersoch but turn left at the T-junction **(Y)**. ½ mile up this steep road come onto the road by the car.

Walk 9 *8 miles*

Abersoch - Llanbedrog - Pwllheli

OS Maps:	1:25 000 *Llŷn Peninsula West Explorer* 12
Start:	Harbour.
Access:	Bus service from Pwllheli.
Parking:	Signposted car parks
Grade:	Moderate: Some short sharp ups & downs and paths not always well maintained.

(-)	denotes Car walk
[-]	denotes Point of interest

Walk directions:

Leaving Abersoch on the A499 Pwllheli road, we take the access path to the beach after crossing the river by the boatyards and, providing the tide is low, we can get round the rocky headland onto the main Warren beach; practically 2 miles of glorious sand. If the tide is in, and in any case dog owners, we carry on along the road until the houses and street lighting end where there is a path through the N.T. sand dunes to the beach. At the far end of the bay, where there is a quarry and the stumps of a one time jetty, there is access to a car park and lane leading away from the sea at the base of the escarpment of Mynydd Tir y Cwmwd (Llanbedrog headland). There is a footpath sign on the right, a few yards along the lane, but as it doesn't appear to lead anywhere but the quarry we can ignore it and carry on for a further 600 yards to a passing place opposite a house Garreg Fawr. The 0.S. shows a path going up the hillside at this point but it is very much overgrown and hardly discernible. Those who are game for a stiff climb and don't mind being scratched by gorse and brambles should look for the start of the path beside the 'Passing Place' sign. After the first steep section of the 'path' comes to a broken wall and strand of barbed wire.

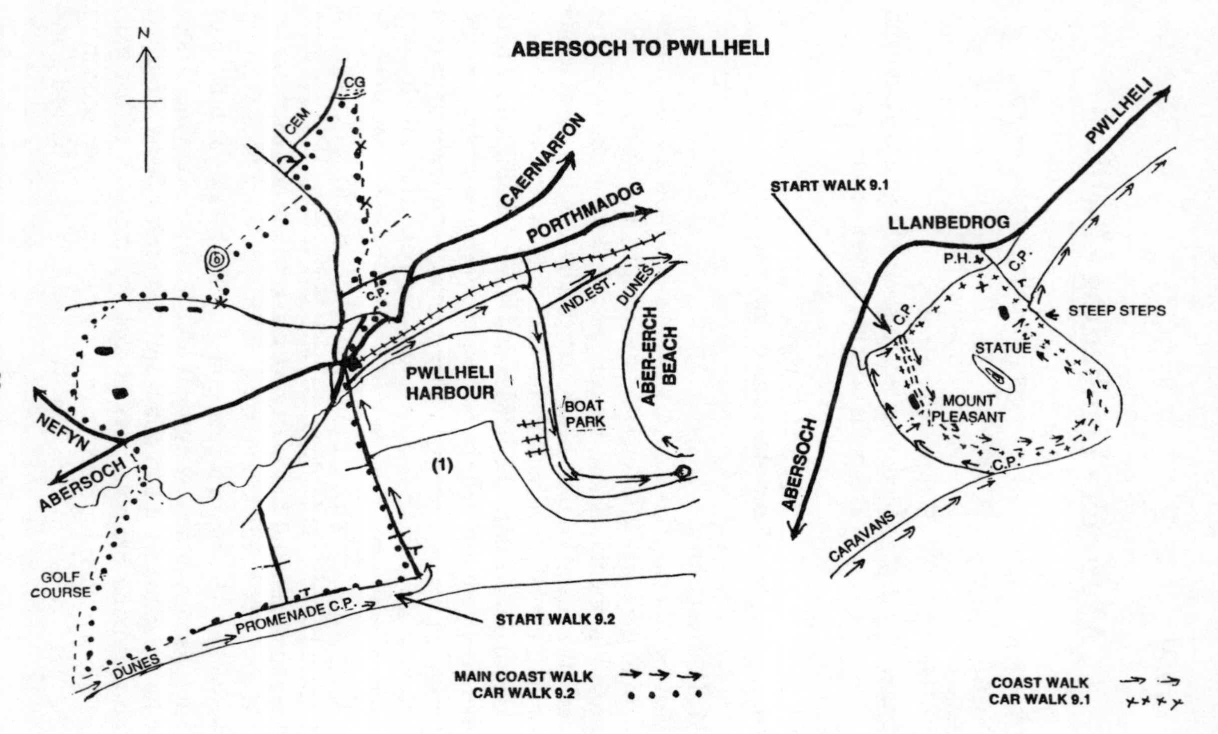
ABERSOCH TO PWLLHELI
N
CEM
CG
CAERNARFON
PORTHMADOG
C.P.
IND.EST.
DUNES
ABER-ERCH BEACH
PWLLHELI HARBOUR
BOAT PARK
(1)
NEFYN
ABERSOCH
GOLF COURSE
PROMENADE C.P.
DUNES
START WALK 9.2
MAIN COAST WALK
CAR WALK 9.2
START WALK 9.1
LLANBEDROG
PWLLHELI
P.H.
C.P.
STEEP STEPS
STATUE
MOUNT PLEASANT
C.P.
ABERSOCH
CARAVANS
COAST WALK
CAR WALK 9.1

Over this it becomes a little easier to the next wall and fence which can be negotiated at the right hand side onto more or less level open ground. In front and slightly to the left is a cottage and buildings known appropriately as 'Mount Pleasant'. Striking half right we join the distinct path which passes in front of this property. Those who wish to take the easier route should carry on up the lane for a further ½ mile where a rough narrow lane goes steeply up to the right, opposite a small car park and which leads to 'Mount Pleasant', **(A)**.

We follow this distinct path round the headland, ignoring turnings that head off towards the summit and being careful not to go too close to the edge for there are sheer drops to the quarry below. Shortly as we come in sight of Llanbedrog beach **(14)** we are confronted by the statue of a man, constructed out of salvaged metal, perched on a rock commanding a view over Pwllheli bay to the mountains of Snowdonia in the distance. Just to the left, a yard or two in front of the tin man there is a narrow path that leads to the very steep and slippery water worn steps descending the cliffs - fortunately there is a handrail for most of the descent. The path passes through an interesting collection of trees in what must have been part of the pleasure grounds of Plas Glyn y Weddw, the Victorian mansion at the foot of the cliff and which now houses an art gallery.

On reaching the bottom we pass round the front of the two storey house onto it's access lane, leaving this to go in front of the picturesque white painted cottage and so reach the lane down to the beach **(B)**. There is a welcome cafe here during the season. A walk along the shore brings us to the rocky headland of Carreg y Defaid which can be negotiated by a fairly easy scramble over the rocks. (In very severe weather it may be necessary to go up the beach approach road, take the first road on the right which comes onto the main road at a garage and in just under ½ mile a cul de sac with access onto the beach.) There is now a 2 mile walk to Pwllheli, either along the beach or, perhaps more pleasantly, just behind the dunes along the trackbed of the old horse drawn tramway that ran from

Pwllheli to Llanbedrog for a number of years in Victorian times. We come out onto the promenade where, at the far end, we turn left and ¼ mile walk along the causeway brings us into the town. Dogs are not allowed on the shore in front of the promenade and must be on a lead at other times.

Pwllheli, **(15)** with a population of 4,000, is the capital of Llŷn peninsula.**[1]** As befits a town of this size all facilities are available.

Points of interest:

[1] It was granted a charter by the Black Prince in 1355 and still holds a popular market on a Wednesday. In 1633 it was terrorised by a pirate ship. Over 400 ships were built here up to 1880, the largest being 700 tons. In 1936, during a Welsh nationalist attack at Penrhos airfield, some 2 miles west of the town, a hangar was burned down in protest of the London government's military manoeuvres on land of heritage importance here in Wales. It was, probably the start of the modern day campaign for Welsh self government. During WW2, this airfield was attacked by German planes on five occasions with the loss of two lives and considerable damage; the Maes (*Square*) in the town was machine gunned on one occasion. Today there is a large marina in the harbour and it is the leading sailing centre in the Irish Sea, hosting such events as the Celtic Regatta and other national and international meetings.

CAR WALKS:

9.1

Description:	A short but healthy walk round Llanbedrog headland with extensive views.
Distance:	2½ miles.
Time:	1½ hours.
Going:	Moderate.
Facilities:	Café and toilets on beach.
Start:	Llanbedrog (325 313)

If coming from Pwllheli on the A499 branch off left at petrol station before entering Llanbedrog, signposted to the Traeth, and follow road round to the right and almost immediately left by St Pedrog church hall. If coming from Abersoch turn right down beside the Glyn-y-Weddw hotel and shortly right by the church hall. This narrow road goes steeply uphill for just over a ¼ mile where there is a small car park on the right.

We join the main walk here **(A)** to go up the lane opposite. On completing the walk round the headland leave the others at the café on the beach **(B)** and go up the tree shaded road to St Pedrog church and turn left. A ¼ mile steady climb brings you back to the car park

9.2

Description:	A walk round Pwllheli the capital of Llŷn with a bird's eye view of town and harbour.
Distance:	4½ miles.
Time:	2 hours.
Going:	Easy.
Facilities:	Café & toilet at either end of promenade: All facilities in the town.
Start:	Pwllheli promenade (375 342).

Free parking is available along the length of the promenade. Until Victorian times this was just a sand bar, separated from the town by the harbour and the Afon Rhyd-hir.

At the west end of the promenade carry on a little further through the sand dunes until turning right just beyond the last house. After 30 yards enter, by a kissing gate, a straight shaded path with the golf course on the left and backs of houses on the right. After 300 yards the path bears right alongside the river (hidden by reeds and wild flowers). Crossing a small wooden footbridge the path then divides. Take the left branch and shortly bear left again over a fine slate slab bridge over the river. The path soon comes out onto the main road by a roundabout.

Taking care cross to the Nefyn road and follow the newly made footpath separated from the road by a low stone wall. Just after the old quarry pass through a wooden gate and turn immediately right through an iron gate onto a grass path that leads uphill through a wood. On emerging the path bends left and then through a farm gate turns right before passing behind a stone barn in the corner of the garden of the big house on the right. It then turns left into a narrow waymarked path through tall grass and brambles. Keeping the hedge on the left and the stone stables across to the right the path rises up to a farm gate into an open field. Keep to the left and, passing an old rusting wind pump, come out onto a road. Turn right and in 500 yards at the top of the hill there is a kissing gate on the left. This grass path emerges into more open ground at the foot of the hill with the trig. point atop. Here the less energetic can carry straight on through the bracken round the northern base of the hill. Others can strike off right to find a way up the hill. Although only just over 200 feet high it gives a stupendous view of the town and new marina. To the south the Cader Idris range across Cardigan Bay; to the north Yr Eifl across fertile farmland.

Descending from the hill in a north easterly direction meet up with the path round the base of the hill to pass through a kissing gate, across a field, down a gravel lane and through another gate onto a road. Turn left and in 30 yards right by a phone box; follow the road round turning right to keep the cemetery wall on the left. Climbing the hill in front passed a chapel on the left and an electricity sub-station on the right, turn right over a cattle grid at Ffridd. As the tarmac drive changes to stone and bears left carry straight on on a difficult to see path through the grass and bracken dropping down to a kissing gate. Cutting across this field to another kissing gate with steps down to the next field. Heading straight across to the far side and dropping down four steps turn right through another gate down a shady path to come out at the back of a block of flats and so onto the street.

Turning left and then almost immediately right into a car park a passage will be found at the far end leading through to the main street. (This passageway is closed at night). Turning right take the first street on the left by the Midland bank which leads to a mini roundabout in the station square. Keep straight ahead along the Cob with the harbour on the left to reach the promenade in just under ½ mile.

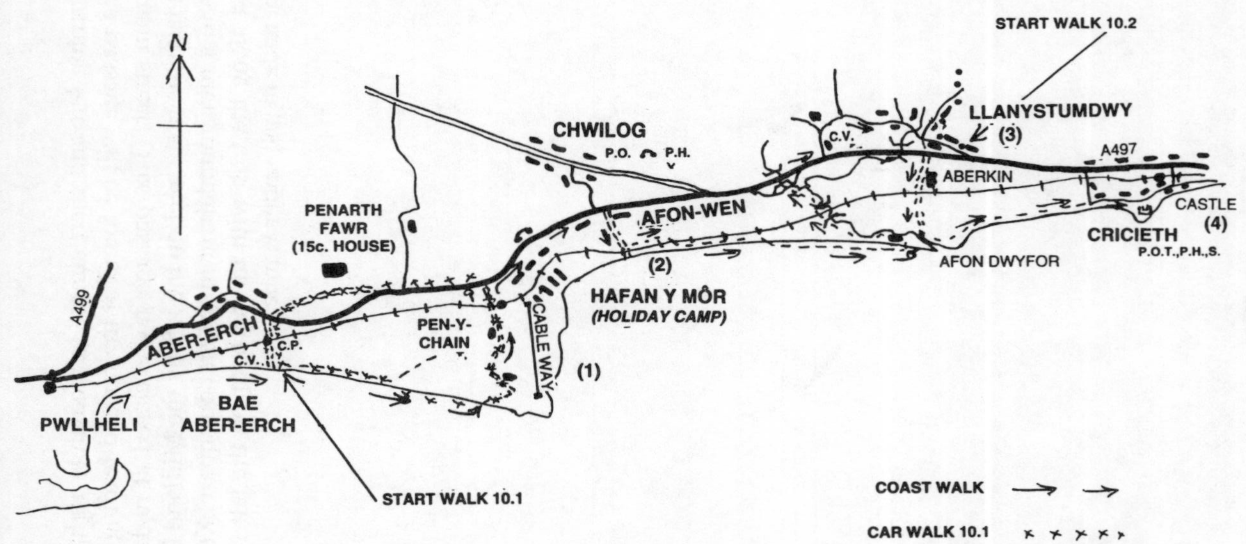

PWLLHELI TO CRICIETH

Walk 10: *13 miles*

Pwllheli - Abererch - Penychain - Afon-wen - Llanystumdwy - Cricieth

OS Maps:	1:25 000 *Llŷn Peninsula East Explorer* 13
Start:	Railway station
Access:	Bus service from Caernarfon. Train from Shrewsbury.
Parking:	Signposted car parks
Grade:	Moderate: Some short sharp ups & downs and paths not always well maintained.

(-) denotes Car walk
[-] denotes Point of interest

Walk directions:

Starting from the station (Pwllheli is the terminus of the Cambrian coast railway built in 1864) take the road down the harbour side, turning right at the end. Those with dogs should take the first turning on the left, through a small industrial estate, and, after 300 yards, a path just to the right of the timber yard in front over the sandhills onto Aberech beach.**(16)** Others, if they wish, can carry on passed the sailing club, admiring the boats in the marina, to the far end where a gate gives onto the beach. This is another 3 mile arc of sand which is rarely busy. Half way along, just passed a hidden caravan site,**(A)** there is a path along the back of the dunes which, according to the O.S., after a further mile heads off inland, but this is best ignored since the exact point where it diverges is uncertain and the hinterland is very wet. Better to continue to the far end where the dunes change to a wide pebble bank, behind which it is easier to walk. Going as far as the rocks there is a path up the low cliff to a kissing gate in the wire fence opening onto the headland of Penychain. Going round the hillock in front, which is actually the wartime remain of rifle butts, we head to another kissing gate in front.**[1]**

We now head for the grass lane in front, making for the white farmhouse Penrhyn. Passing through the two gates of the yard we follow the winding farm access lane until the next farm, Penychain. (After leaving Penrhyn don't follow the path shown on the O.S. that bears off right – keep to the lane). Carrying on down the lane we come to the recently rebuilt Penychain station, where holiday makers and sailors used to arrive in their thousands for the Butlins camp, now under new management and called Hafan y Môr. Here we have to make a decision. The route forward to Cricieth involves some walking on a busy main road and is, we must admit, the least enjoyable of the whole walk. The railway is handy and by this stage there must be a temptation to take a break, so why not indulge and put your feet up as far as Cricieth. If interested in this suggestion enquiries should be made at Pwllheli station so as to time arrival. Trains are not frequent but there is usually one about 3 o'clock and another at 5 o'clock.

For those purists who consider this as cheating and wish to complete the whole walk on foot, then carry on up the lane a further 100 yards **(B)** and turn right on the main road passed the main entrance to Hafan y Môr. Continuing down the road for just under a mile to a row of houses where we turn right, down the cul de sac lane, at the end of the terrace. Just before passing under the railway bridge we go over the bridge on the left and up to the railway, crossing the line, to gain the sea wall. **[2]**

We follow the sea wall until the railway veers inland when we have to take to the beach. After ¾ mile we come to the isolated house Ty'n y Morfa which overlooks the beach. There is a kissing gate into the field, at the far side of which is Afon Dwyfor. The map shows a path crossing the river at this point, and we understand that there is a causeway beneath the surface, though not visible, and we would certainly not recommend trying to use it. At very low tides it is sometimes possible to wade across the mouth of the river on the beach, but the other, and more certain way, is to follow the river upstream, and to this end there is a stile in the N.W. corner of the field, behind the house with a path leading up to the railway line which it crosses by another stile. If there was an official path across the railway bridge we could regain the opposite bank avoiding a 2 mile detour. The alternative is to follow the path northwards through the woods and then down some steps into the field on the right. Keeping to the left a gate leads out onto the old road and then turning right we join the main road, crossing to the pavement on the other side. 500 yards along we can take a short but interesting diversion into the village of Llanystumdwy.**[3]** Another ½ mile crossing back over the main road to go down the farm lane to Aberkin. After passing the farm the lane continues over a stile then bearing left and then right to recross the railway. The lane now leads, through a gate in front, into a field at the very far corner of which a stile finally takes us out onto the river bank.

This track can get flooded at very high tides and thus is a bit messy. At the mouth of the river the path on top of the bank has been washed away so that we have to walk round the small headland on the stony beach before regaining the path. Following the now clear path for ¾ mile brings us out onto Cricieth **(17)** west promenade. This last section of this path is subject to erosion and could well be diverted. A short walk along the promenade brings us to Cricieth castle.**[4]** Dropping down to the east promenade, pass Cadwalader's well known ice cream shop, take the street opposite which leads into the town centre.

With a population of 1,700 and a popular holiday resort, particularly with older people, Cricieth is well supplied with hotels, restaurants etc. Dogs are not allowed on either beach.

Points of interest:

[1] This headland is part of the Hafan y Môr holiday camp complex and it is understandable that all and sundry cannot be allowed to walk through it, so that we have to turn inland. However a short detour up to the trig. point is probably permissible and will be rewarded with fine views to Cricieth in front, to Pwllheli behind and across Bae Ceredigion (*Cardigan Bay*) to Harlech and Bermo (*Barmouth*). Scattered around the headland are relics of gun emplacements – a reminder that, during the last war, the camp was known as H.M.S. Glendower, a gunnery training ship of which many ex sailors, including the Duke of Edinburgh, will have 'fond' memories.

[2] This was Afon-wen junction and it is hard to imagine now that, up until 1964, when the line coming in from Caernarfon was closed and it's raisin d'être went, that this station once boasted three platforms, a licensed refreshment room and at peak periods handled 17 trains a day in each direction. Now all that remains, apart from the Cambrian coast track, are the outlines of the old platform, sidings and the station master's bungalow.

[3] The lifetime home of Lloyd George, the WW1 Prime Minister and statesman, by taking the road on the left. This leads down to the old bridge over Afon Dwyfor, on the bank of which, just upstream , he is buried in a grave designed by Clough Williams Ellis.There is also a museum. Members of the nearby Baptist Chapel are still baptised under the bridge. Immediately after crossing the bridge we take a path on the right, behind the houses to rejoin the main road, crossing to the farm lane opposite.

[4] Cricieth Castle – built by the Welsh, in the 13th.C. it was improved by Edward 1 and finally taken by Owain Glyndŵr in 1404.

CAR WALKS:

10.1

Description:	A fine beach; a holiday camp with wartime memories; return via a leafy lane with some good views. (There is an unavoidable ½ mile stretch along a busy main road).
Distance:	5 miles.
Time:	2½ hours.
Going:	Moderate.
Facilities:	None.
Start:	Abererch station. (404 362)

Just 2 miles out of Pwllheli, on the A497 Cricieth road, take the minor road on the right with signs to Abererch Holiday Park and station. Over the level crossing there is a free car park on the right.

Walk towards the dunes and join the main walk at this point **(A)**, either along the path at the back of the dunes or along the beach.

Having followed the main directions round as far as Butlins **(B)** turn left on the main road. This is a busy road without a footpath, so take care. In ½ mile the road bends sharply left but go straight ahead onto a rough road which follows the stone wall of the Broom Hall estate. This pleasant lane leads, in just under a mile, back onto the main road. Turn right and, in 200 yards, cross and go back down the road to the car park.

10.2

Description:	A wooded river bank walk with reminders of a former elder statesman.
Distance:	4½ miles.
Time:	2½ hours.
Going:	Moderate but muddy in places; boots recommended.
Facilities:	Café & toilets in village.
Start:	Llanystumdwy (475 385)

LLANYSTUMDWY – AFON DWYFOR

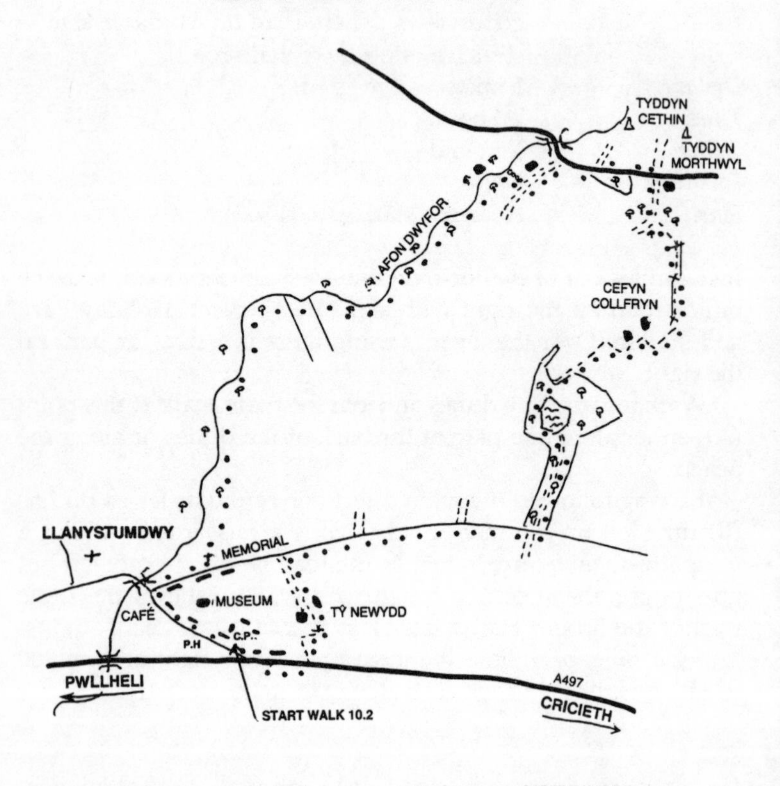

Llanystumdwy lies just off the main road less than 2 miles west of Cricieth. There is a free car park by the council houses Cricieth side of the village. This is Lloyd George territory, with his old cobbler cottage home recently restored to its former character and reopened to the public.

Turn right out of the car park, passed the little cottage where the great man spent his early life. Pass the museum and turn right just before the bridge. In 50 yards, take the path on the left by L.G's burial site overlooking Afon Dwyfor designed by Clough Williams Ellis of Portmeirion fame. Drop down to the river and follow this pretty wooded path as it meanders along its bank. In 1½ miles come to a stone wall with a stile in front but ignore this and follow the wall up to the right to pass through a stone arch onto a lane.

Turn left and follow the lane to the main road. Turn right and proceed up the road for 500 yards to turn right down a rough lane by a house with signpost to Cricieth. After a few yards branch off left, through the trees, to a kissing gate into a field. Keep to the left of this field to another kissing gate in the corner and then turn right to follow the other side of the fence to yet another kissing gate. The next mile or so is a little difficult since the path shown on the O.S. has been more or less obliterated. However keeping the fence on the right come to a farm track at the far side of the field and turn right to shortly enter, through a gate, the farm yard of Cefncollfryn. Turn left down the near gable end of the farm buildings and through a gate onto another rough farm lane which very soon turns right to enter a field. Turn left and keeping first the low stone wall and then the wood on the left proceed down to the corner of the field. Here it becomes very marshy and although there are signs that there was once a gate it has now been fenced off. The fence on the left is easier to climb to enter the wood. Here there is no sign of a path and it is a question of fighting ones way through the trees continuing, as far as possible, in a straight line with the edge of the field just traversed.

After a few yards it is surprising to find a sign *'Private fishing. Dogs loose'* but no apparent place where one is not supposed to fish! However bearing left just after this notice press on through the undergrowth and finally arrive at the said fishing spot hidden in the trees. Follow round the south side of this small lake, passed a hut and caravan to leave the area by the rough drive which leads onto the minor road opposite the entrance to Broneifion Farm.

Turn right and in just over ½ mile take the driveway on the left to Tŷ Newydd, L.G's main home in the village. Follow the drive round between the house and some converted cottages and leave by a kissing gate in front. Turn immediately right to a stone stile into the next field. (good view of the garden and house from here). Keep to the left of this field to emerge onto the main road. Turn right and shortly bear right back to the car park.

Walk 11 *6 miles*

Cricieth - Black Rock Sands - Morfa Bychan - Borth-y-Gest - Porthmadog

OS Maps:	1:25 000 *Llŷn Peninsula East Explorer* 13
Start:	Far end of the east promenade
Access:	Bus service from Caernarfon. Train from Shrewsbury, Pwllheli
Parking:	East promenade
Grade:	Moderate: Some short sharp ups & downs and paths not always well maintained.

(-)	denotes Car walk
[-]	denotes Point of interest

Walk directions:

We start this, the final leg of our walk, at the far end of the east promenade by the 1920's style cafe. Just before the level crossing there is a footpath which runs alongside the railway behind the cafe. After ½ mile the path crosses the line and, ignoring the stile in front we continue alongside the track. From here there is a good view back towards the castle. Ignoring the next stile on the left **(A)**. Keep on alongside the line, rounding the rock outcrop actually on the track. Here we must say that, due to tidal currents and winds, there is an enormous amount of plastic detritus which makes the place messy. The path drops below the level of the line but there are fine views inland to the distant mountains and a number of ponds with wildlife. A little further on, as the railway turns inland, the path once again crosses it to a white painted stile into open ground.**(B)** Now we head towards the seaward side of the rocky hill – Graig Ddu, and scrambling round the headland we bear slightly upwards

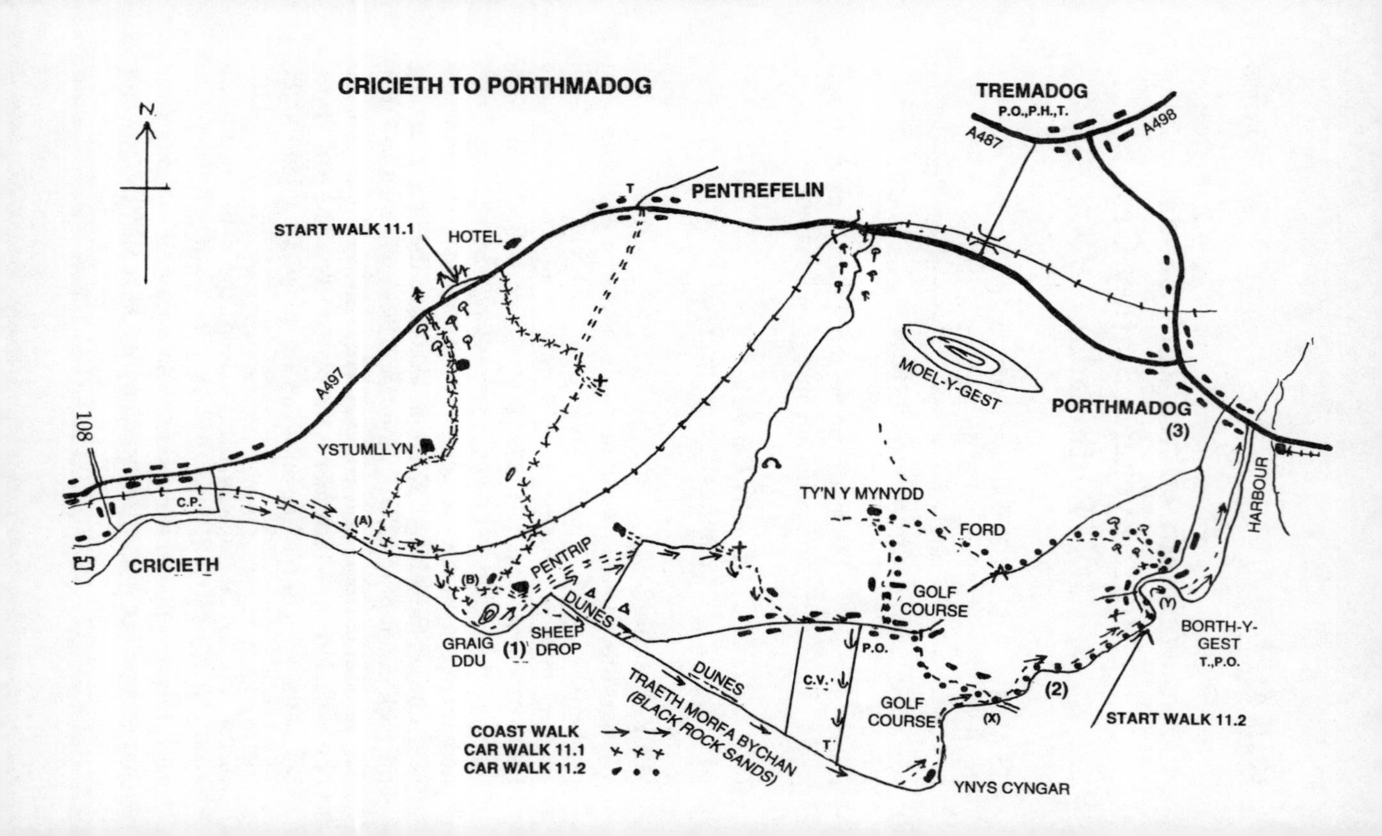
CRICIETH TO PORTHMADOG
N
START WALK 11.1
HOTEL
T
PENTREFELIN
TREMADOG
P.O.,P.H.,T.
A487
A498
A497
YSTUMLLYN
MOEL-Y-GEST
PORTHMADOG
(3)
HARBOUR
C.P.
(A)
CRICIETH
(B)
PENTRIP
DUNES
TY'N Y MYNYDD
FORD
GOLF
COURSE
GRAIG
DDU
(1)
SHEEP
DROP
P.O.
C.V.
T
DUNES
TRAETH MORFA BYCHAN
(BLACK ROCK SANDS)
GOLF
COURSE
(X)
(2)
(Y)
BORTH-Y-
GEST
T.,P.O.
START WALK 11.2
YNYS CYNGAR
COAST WALK
CAR WALK 11.1
CAR WALK 11.2

where the cliffs become sheer, to a wall and fence. We are now looking down on the two mile stretch of Black Rock sands.**(18)**. There are no clear paths here and the fence must be negotiated at the most convenient point. We now have to find our way through the gorse in a half left direction to the top of the cliff where there is a narrow cleft in the rock leading to the beach. Negotiating this is not for the faint hearted and requires both hands and great care. There is a final drop of 7 or 8 feet onto soft sand.**[1]** There is no other way down the cliff and if this route is considered too difficult turn back up to the open ground of Graig Ddu and head, in the field behind the caravans, towards the farm buildings of Pentrip where a farm lane leads to a narrow road. Turning down this road and left at the bottom in 200 yards come to the access to the sands on the right.

Dogs are not allowed on this section of the shore so for an alternative route, instead of turning right down the road, go straight on up the road. After ¼ mile there is a small church on the right in the far corner of which a kissing gate into a small field with another in front. Go through this and follow the left of the field down to the farm Glan-y-morfa-mawr.There are good views from here across the Glaslyn estuary to Harlech and the mountains beyond. Keeping the farm on the left cut down through the caravan site below out onto the road.Turn left and after ½ mile turn right, just before the Spar shop down the straight road that leads directly onto the beach to join up with those who have walked along the sands.

Walking along the sands as far as the rocky outcrop of Ynys Cyngar as we approach it there is a path, just behind the lifebuoy and warning sign, leading up the hill and passing behind the house of that name. The N.T. have thoughtfully provided a board walk through the dunes to the sea defence wall with the golf course on our left. Following the path round the bay and after crossing a slipway **(X)** quickly turn left to climb the wooden steps up the steep cliff. Nearing the top, where the path divides, we keep to the right up a few concrete steps with handrail and the path levels out. On coming to a dirt road we pass through the gate on the right and immediately turn left with the footpath sign. A few yards further on, just before a house up on the left, we take the path down to the right. This leads onto a pleasant sandy cliff top walk. **[2]**

Later the path has been covered by sand and we slide down to the small sandy cove with rock outcrops. Beware of the strong currents here. Climbing the steps at the far side and following the boardwalk, ignoring, first a path coming in on the left and then one with a handrail going down to the right, we finally arrive at a headland with a number of viewpoint seats and a church on the left. Joining now the metalled road which curves left and then becomes the promenade of Borth y Gest.**(19)** This sleepy village once had four shipbuilders.**(Y)**.

At the far end of the curved promenade we take the footpath and steps up to the right of the building in front. This comes out on a road of superior detached houses and ignoring the road that comes in on the right and where the road bears off left we keep straight ahead down an unmade road which soon becomes just a path leading down to the boatyards. Turning left at the bottom a ¼ mile level walk brings us to Porthmadog harbour, which marks the end of our journey.**[3]** The town, with a population of some 2,000, has all the usual facilities.

Points of interest:

[1] In 1907 the *Owen Morris*, almost home from Labrador, was wrecked here.

[2] Fine views across the estuary to the Rhinog mountains and, further up the estuary, the causeway (The Cob) built by Wm. Maddocks in 1811 to reclaim 7,000 acres of land, at the same time establishing the town of Porthmadog. From this point it is easy to see the difficulties sailors had, indeed still have, in navigating the narrow course of the river, but what cannot be seen is the submerged hazard of Sarn Badrig (*St Patrick's* *causeway*) which extends for several miles in a S.W. direction from Harlech, and on which many a vessel has foundered.

[3] Porthmadog harbour opened in 1824 and came into its own in 1836 when the Ffestiniog railway came into the town across the Cob. At first the line operated by gravity, horses travelling down by truck to haul the empties back up, but in 1863 steam engines were introduced. It is the oldest narrow gauge railway and is today the most successful tourist attraction carrying thousands the 12 miles up to Blaenau Ffestiniog where there is a link with the standard rail down the Conwy valley to Llandudno.

The vast quantities of slate produced by the huge quarries of Blaenau were exported all over the world but they built up a considerable trade with Germany particularly after the great fire of Hamburg in 1842. In 1873 100,000 tons of slate were exported through the port. Naturally many of the ships carrying this cargo were built locally – more than 300 in Porthmadog. With the general decline in shipbuilding in the 1880's Porthmadog was alone in carrying on into the 2Oth.C. building fine schooners, known as Western Ocean Yachts, renowned the world over. Shipbuilding finally ended in 1914.

Across the estuary is Portmeirion, the fantasy village built by the famous architect, Sir Clough Williams Ellis where the T.V. drama 'The Prisoner' was filmed. A mile inland is the village of Tremadog, laid out by Wm. Maddocks and the birth place of Lawrence of Arabia.

CAR WALKS:

11.1

Description: A pleasant country walk with fine views all around; an interesting church.

Distance: 3 miles.

Time: 2 hours.

Going: Moderate but very wet & muddy over part of the route; boots essential.

Facilities: None.
Start: Pentrefelin (518 391)

1½ miles out of Cricieth on the A497 Porthmadog road there is a small lay-by on the left where the road enters the trees and just before the Plas Gwyn hotel.

Cross the road and turn right back towards Cricieth and in 100 yards turn left down the wooded drive to Ystumllyn. There are some fine specimen trees in this wood. Follow the drive round behind what has obviously been a fine house to emerge, over a cattle grid and kissing gate into open country. Follow the drive up into the farmyard and keeping to the left of the buildings pass through the stile and gate in front. Keeping the fence and wall on the left pass through the left hand of the two gates in front, with the fence now on the right.

From here there is a magnificent view of the attractive Victorian resort of Cricieth, dominated by its castle. Again take the left one of the next two gates and still with the fence on the right but going straight ahead when it turns sharply right, drop down an indistinct farm track to a shallow gorge with the pebble beach in front the other side of the railway. A stile leads onto the path alongside the railway and turning left join the main walk. **(A)**

Crossing back over the railway at point **(B)**, instead of following the main walk round the seaward side of the headland in front, take the obvious farm track which goes round the northern side and nearing the top there is a cottage in a knot of trees on the left. The route goes through the farm gate alongside the cottage but before doing so carry on up the farm track for 100 yards or so to get a stupendous view looking down on the vast expanse of Black Rock sands. The more energetic can climb to the top of Graig Ddu for an even better view.

Returning to the cottage go through the gate and follow down and round into a field by a caravan. The route from here for the next mile is not obvious and not helped by the sign

'Beware of the bull' and *'Private'*. In the absence of any more obvious path keep to the right of this field, passed the caravan, and keeping to the base of the crag drop down to the railway where an underpass in the corner leads out onto the open wetlands beyond. The next ½ mile is very wet but negotiable with proper footwear.

From the underpass go straight ahead until the river is reached. Turn left along its bank and in a few yards an overgrown footbridge crosses to the other side. A cart track now crosses the path and the drainage ditch on the right must be crossed at this point. (the path straight ahead looks inviting but leads to trouble). Having crossed the ditch keep round the left of this field to a sort of stile by a clump of stunted trees in the far corner. This corner is very muddy but there is a gate just to the right which is drier. Now carry on along the next wetland with the hedge on the right – in spring this is a carpet of yellow iris – to come out through a gate onto a tarmac lane.

Turning right in 100 yards or so is the interesting old Victorian church of Ynyscynhaearn with a fine stone lychgate and, inside box pews and a three decker pulpit. One wonders where the congregation came from since the nearest habitation is ¾ mile away, but judging by the memorials and headstones it was indeed a prosperous one. This tranquil church is no longer used for services except the occasional funeral. The old graveyard, now very much overgrown, warrants further inspection.

Returning down the lane for 300 yards find a small gated stile on the left. Keeping the field wall on the left pass through another gate and then going straight ahead to another gate and stile. The vague path ahead leads to a stile out on to the main road almost opposite the car.

11.2

Description: Interesting walk through woods and open hillside to return along Afon Glaslyn estuary to the tiny resort of Borth-y-Gest.

Distance:	3 miles.
Time:	2 hours.
Going:	Moderate.
Facilities:	Shops, café & toilets by car park.
Start:	Borth-y-Gest (565 374)

From Porthmadog turn up beside Woolworths, half way along the main street. In just over ½ mile fork left signposted to Borth-y-Gest. Car park at the far end of the promenade.

Walk back along the prom. and go up the lane between the two modern houses next to the Ebenezer chapel half way along at the top of which a flight of stone steps leads up to a gate into a field. Straight across the field another gate leads into a wood of fine straight oak trees. Since at the end of the last century ships were built on the beach perhaps these trees were planted for a purpose. Follow the obvious path through the wood to finally come out on a road. Turn left and just over the brow of the hill look for a stile and footpath sign on the right. Follow this wide grass track as it winds along passed a small lake on the left to drop down to a gate and ford. A path here goes off up to the right but keep ahead on the wide track with the mass of Moel-y-Gest to the right, and after passing through a gate reach the isolated house Ty'n-y-Mynydd.

Now, by the electricity pole at the house turn back to follow the line of the poles down hill. After the third pole go over the waymarked stile just to the right and by the next pole look for a narrow path on the right which leads down the low cliff to the rather wet ground below. Carry on straight ahead to a footbridge across a stream and in twenty or so yards, by a waymarker, cross a ford to the right and then swing round to the left to arrive at a stile above farm buildings in front. Pass through the buildings leaving by the track that crosses the golf course to emerge on the road at Morfa Bychan.

Turn left and in 100 yards turn right by the golf clubhouse with a finger post to Borth-y-Gest. Follow the dirt road round the golf course and by the last house on the left go down the narrow path in front which leads to a small slipway. This is now part of the main walk **(X)** and follow those directions back to the car park **(Y)**.

CONCLUSION

The return to Caernarfon can be made by bus across the neck of the peninsula. The Ffestiniog Railway are in the process of restoring the old Welsh Highland Railway line through the heart of Snowdonia, from Porthmadog to Caernarfon and when this is completed will make a fitting end to the walk. At present they have only restored the line from Caernarfon to Dinas just over two miles.

It is to be hoped that those who have completed the journey will have derived a great deal of satisfaction from it and that this little book will have been of assistance and interest. Perhaps it might encourage others to discover the beauties of the Llŷn peninsula and in so doing encourage the N.T. and the local authority to bring those parts of the walk to which we are at present denied access into the route. In most cases there is ample space on the cliff tops outside the fencing for a path and it is a shame that these cannot be opened up for the benefit of all to enjoy it.

MILEAGES

Caernarfon	to	Dinas Dinlle	11 miles
Dinas Dinlle	to	Trefor	11
Trefor	to	Nefyn	9
Nefyn	to	Tudweiliog	9
Tudweiliog	to	Anelog	10½
(Anelog	to	Aberdaron direct	1½
Anelog	to	Aberdaron	7½
Aberdaron	to	Llanengan	11
Llanengan	to	Abersoch	9
Abersoch	to	Pwllheli	8
Pwllheli	to	Cricieth	13
Cricieth	to	Porthmadog	6

Total 105 miles.

GLOSSARY

Aber	*River mouth*	Afon	*River*
Bach	*Little*	Bryn	*Hill*
Bwlch	*Pass or col.*	Cae	*Field*
Caer	*Fort*	Capel	*Chapel*
Carreg	*Stone*	Coed	*Wood*
Croes	*Cross*	Cwm	*Valley*
Ffordd	*Road*	Ffynnon	*Well*
Heddlu	*Police*	Isaf	*Lower*
Llan	*Church area*	Llyn	*Lake*
Maen	*Stone*	Maes	*Town square*
Mawr	*Big*	Moel	*Bare mountain*
Morfa	*Sea-marsh*	Mynydd	*Mountain*
Nant	*Valley*	Newydd	*New*
Penrhyn	*Headland*	Pistyll	*Waterfall*
Plas	*Large house*	Porth	*Harbour*
Pont	*Bridge*	Pwll	*Pool*
Sarn	*Causeway*	Stryd	*Street*
Traeth	*Beach*	Tŷ	*House*
Uchaf	*Upper*	Ynys	*Island*
Ysbyty	*Hospital*	Ysgol	School

BEST BEACH GUIDE.

The Llŷn peninsula is justly proud of its many fine beaches. Here are listed 19 of the best. As walkers round the coast will have found there are very many more idyllic coves that we could not possibly list, most of them being inaccessible except on foot.

In line with the main text these 19 beaches are listed anti-clockwise round the peninsula. Further information can be found against the appropriate number in the main text.

The question of classifying the beaches in the area has yet to be fully resolved. Blue Flag beaches are those which conform to the very strict guidelines laid down by the E.C. Apart from water quality ,sampled on a regular basis, they list 26 other criteria such as provision of toilets, fresh water, lifesaving equipment, telephone, general cleanliness etc. etc. A number of beaches have qualified for a Seaside Award, the criteria for which have been laid down by the U.K. authorities and are only slightly less stringent than the E.C. guidelines. These beaches fly a blue/yellow flag and currently include Aberdaron. All these awards are reviewed annually and can be withdrawn if standards are not maintained. Having read a synopsis of these criteria it is doubtful if many of the smaller beaches will be able, or indeed would necessarily want, to comply. After all, most people only want to know whether the water is clean and the beach safe. However it is hoped to include Cricieth and Morfa Bychan (Black Rock sands) in the list of Blue Flag beaches by the year 2,000.

Apart from this, all interested parties have got together to form a Green Sea Initiative by which it is hoped to provide recognition for the quality of some 80 beaches in Wales that are too remote or ineligible for Blue Flag status.

In describing the state of beaches it is important to note that they can change overnight as a result of rough weather. The

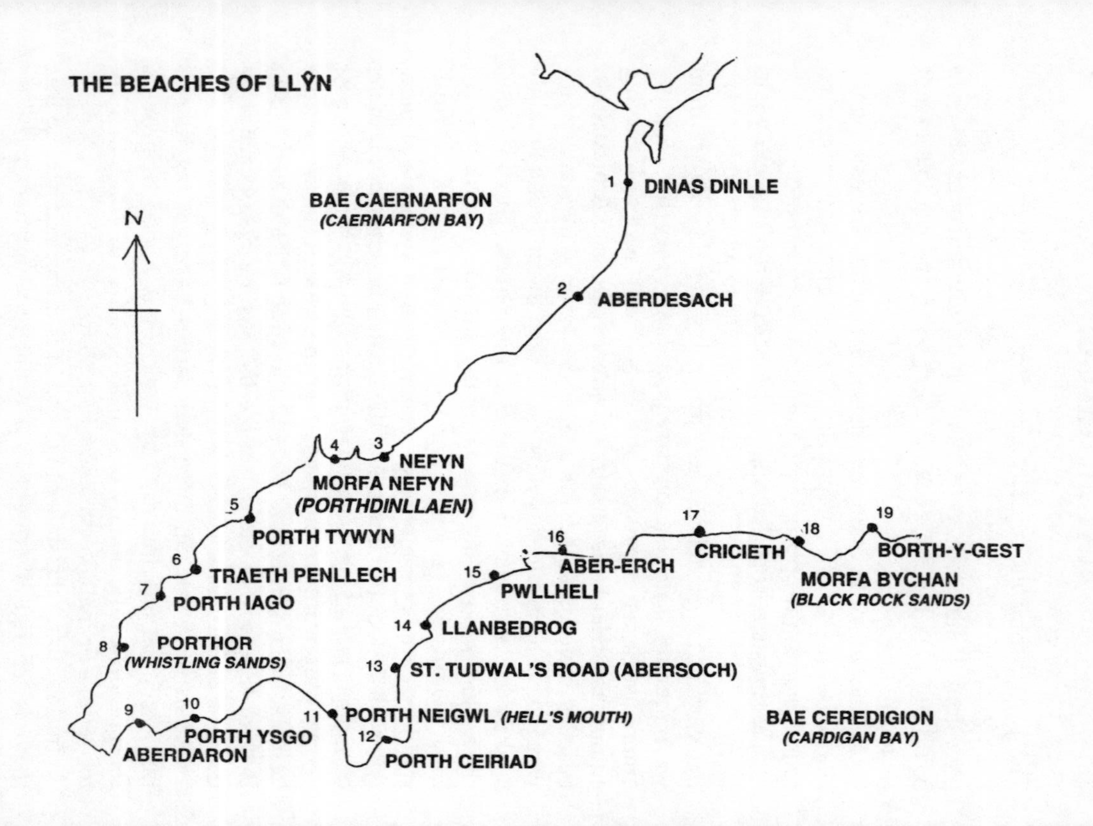
THE BEACHES OF LLŶN
N
BAE CAERNARFON
(CAERNARFON BAY)
1 DINAS DINLLE
2 ABERDESACH
3 NEFYN
4 MORFA NEFYN
(PORTHDINLLAEN)
5 PORTH TYWYN
6 TRAETH PENLLECH
7 PORTH IAGO
8 PORTHOR
(WHISTLING SANDS)
9 ABERDARON
10 PORTH YSGO
11 PORTH NEIGWL (HELL'S MOUTH)
12 PORTH CEIRIAD
13 ST. TUDWAL'S ROAD (ABERSOCH)
14 LLANBEDROG
15 PWLLHELI
16 ABER-ERCH
17 CRICIETH
18 MORFA BYCHAN
(BLACK ROCK SANDS)
19 BORTH-Y-GEST
BAE CEREDIGION
(CARDIGAN BAY)

description given is that for their normal state as currently known. Dogs are banned from certain beaches from May 1st. to 31st. September as indicated. At all times and all beaches owners are expected to clean up.

Finally a few do's and don'ts for safety at the seaside.

1. Do keep a watchful eye on all the family (and indeed others) at all times. Even rock pools can be a hazard to small children.
2. Don't use inflatables unless attached to a long rope.
3. Do make sure you have an escape route should the tide come in unexpectedly.
4. Don't swim after a heavy meal or drinking.
5. Do heed warning signs.
6. Don't swim in rough conditions or near headlands.
7. Finally a word to water skiers and water bikers; please have consideration for the safety and comfort of others and use the special areas where designated.

1. DINAS DINLLE (436 566)

Description:	This beach is a 2 mile stretch of sand backed by a pebble bank and coast protection wall. Faces west and can be a little exposed. Sand dunes beyond north end ideal for sunbathing.
Facilities:	Seaside shops, cafes and phone at south end. Toilets at either end and in the centre. Picnic tables. Museum and restaurant at airport.
Directions:	1½ miles off A499 Caernarfon to Pwllheli road at Llandwrog; 5 miles from Caernarfon; 14 miles from Pwllheli and Nefyn.
Parking:	Free along the foreshore.
Dogs:	Not allowed on first 1/3 of beach.

2. ABERDESACH (425 514)

Description: ¼ mile stretch of sand at low tide backed by pebble bank. Faces west and little or no shelter.

Facilities: Seasonal 'portaloo' Picnic tables phone on main road. Small boats can be launched.

Directions: Just off the A499 12 miles north of Pwllheli and Nefyn.

Parking: Free on foreshore.

3. NEFYN (305 405)

Description: 1½ miles of sand. The west part of the beach backed by concrete retaining wall culminating in a tiny harbour. The east part backed by pebble bank and high cliffs subject to landslip .Although north facing high cliffs provide protection from S. and W. winds. Popular with windsurfers and canoeists. Rarely crowded .

Facilities: All available in the village ½ mile away. Toilets and shop on beach. Public slipway with seasonal charge for launching. Dinghy sailing club operates during high season. Beach huts for hire.

Directions: ¼ mile out of village on B4417. Road to beach 2nd. On right opposite school.

Parking: Limited at bottom of screw road; large free park 100 yards right on main road.

Dogs: Not allowed on western section.

4. MORFA NEFYN – PORTHDINLLAEN (282 405)

Description: Really three beaches. The main 1½ miles of sand backed by grass covered cliffs to left; pebble bank & coast protection rocks to right. Rarely crowded. Can be problems with water skiers who tend to ignore designated safety lanes. Further round bay small sandy beach of Porthdinllaen. Popular for pub on beach and for messing around in boats. Crowded in high season. Further round path at foot of cliffs is lifeboat bay. A tiny cove of very clean sand and water split by the lifeboat slipway. Always a sheltered spot and only used by those in the know. A long drag from the car park but well worth the effort - and there is always the pub half way!

Facilities: Inn & toilets at bottom of approach road and at Porthdinllaen. Public slipway with seasonal charge for launching. Lifeboat.

Directions: 1¼ miles from Nefyn on B4417 fork right at diagonal X-roads in Morfa Nefyn. For beach turn right by Linksway hotel.

Parking: Limited free on approach road. N.T. pay car park at foot of golf approach road. near Linksway hotel with steps in far right corner to beach. NOTE: There is no vehicular access to either Porthdinllaen or Lifeboat beaches.

Dogs: Banned from the beach to the right of the slipway otherwise no problem.

5. PORTH TYWYN (232 375)

Description: 2 small, beautiful sandy beaches backed by grass cliffs between rocky headlands.

Facilities: None.

Directions: Turn right just before entering village of Tudweiliog on the B4417 just under 4 miles from Morfa Nefyn. Follow road round to Towyn farm. Beach is across the field opposite.

Parking: In field by farm Honesty box.

Dogs: Banned from the main beach.

6. TRAETH PENLLECH (205 345)

Description: A mile long stretch of clean sand backed by pebbles and high grass cliffs with rocky outcrops providing sheltered corners and rock pools. Plenty of space for the few visitors.

Facilities: None.

Directions: Turn right just before the P.O. in Llangwnnadl on the B4417. Turn right at the X-roads for ½ mile.

Parking: Good free parking on road above, on the left by a stream. To get to beach cross bridge and take path on left through two fields.

Dogs: No problems.

7. PORTH IAGO (167 316)

Description: Narrow sandy beach between rocky headlands. Sheltered sun trap. An easy scramble down sand & grass cliff the actual shore. Being small and popular can get a little crowded at height of season.

Facilities: None.

Directions: Fork right off the B4413 just after Penygroeslon signposted to Porthor (*Whistling Sands*). After 2 miles turn right at the cluster of buildings at Methlem. At next farm, Tŷ Hen, turn left with sign to Porth Iago. A short way down turn left down farm track to Tŷ Mawr farm and beyond to headland.

Parking: On headland above beach. Honesty box at farm.

8. PORTHOR (Whistling Sands) (165 300)

Description: A wide fine sandy beach between rocky headlands and backed by grass cliffs.

Owned by N.T. The dry sand wh
walked on.
Popular and can get busy.

Facilities: Beach café & toilet.

Directions: As for Porth Iago but bear left with road at Methlem farm. Approach lane to beach ¾ mile on right.

Parking: Paid parking on approach lane. 200 yard steepish walk down to shore.

Dogs: Not allowed.

9. ABERDARON (172 264)

Description: A mile long stretch of sand backed by the village and sandy cliffs. Popular but size prevents it becoming crowded. This is a blue/yellow flag beach.

Facilities: Though tiny the village boasts 2 hotels, a couple of cafes , shops, P.O. & toilets.

Directions: Virtually at the end of the peninsula and approached by the B4413

Parking: Paid parking on the right just before the bridge in the village.

Dogs: Not permitted on the right (western) side.

10. PORTH YSGO (208 265)

Description: Small secluded sandy cove backed by high grass cliffs . Covered at high tide. Waterfall. Difficult access - ½ mile from road and steep wooden steps down to shore - ensures it never gets crowded. Owned by N.T.

Facilities: None.

Directions: On the secondary road from Rhiw to Aberdaron one mile from the former turn left at the X-roads at Groeslon forking right at the bottom.

Parking: Either in small lay-by at the fork or further along at Ysgo farm. Signed footpaths to the beach from either place.
Dogs: Accepted.

11. PORTH NEIGWL (Hell's Mouth) (284 265)

Description: A 4 mile stretch of sand mostly covered at high tide, backed by sand & clay cliffs subject to landslips; dunes towards the eastern end. Its vast length ensures it is usually deserted. Exposed to any wind with south in it. Bathing can be dangerous particularly in rough seas there is a strong undertow . More a beach for walking.
Facilities: None.
Directions: From Abersoch follow signs for Llanengan. In village go straight ahead and in ½ mile keep right and entrance to beach is 200 yards on left.
Parking: Free at entrance to beach.
Dogs: No problem.

12. PORTH CEIRIAD (311 248)

Description: A popular beach owned by N.T. Sand backed by high grass cliffs with steps down. Neighbouring caravan sites ensure a fair number of visitors in season, though its mile length gives plenty of space
Facilities: None. Emergency phone on cliff top.
Directions: From Abersoch take the road to Sarn Bach and go straight at X-roads in the hamlet and in ¾ mile take narrow road on the left which leads to Nant-y-big farm.
Parking: Paid in Nant-y-big farm then path down to cliff top.
Dogs: Accepted.

13. ST TUDWAL'S ROAD – ABERSOCH (315 282)

Description: Probably the most popular resort on the peninsula. This 3 mile stretch of sand is in effect two beaches divided by Afon Soch and the town itself. Borth Fawr, the south beach is the more popular and for many years the sailing centre of the peninsula. The Warren, or northern beach is backed by an extensive holiday chalet complex but is usually quieter and possibly has finer sand. Both beaches are backed by dunes. Borth Fawr, because of the sailing fraternity can become crowded during the season.

Facilities: Abersoch itself has all the usual holiday facilities. The south beach has shop, café & toilet by the headland that separates the two beaches. The Warren has none. There are launching slipways in the harbour & over the sands. Beach huts available. Inshore lifeboat.

Directions: Abersoch is 6½ miles south of Pwllheli on the A499.

Parking: There are at least 5 parking areas serving the beaches. At the bottom of the minor road at the foot of Llanbedrog headland at the far end of the Warren: on the roadside verge just before entering the town: behind the sailing club in the centre: by the golf club: and at the south end of Borth Fawr.

Dogs: Banned from the harbour round to the golf club.

14. LLANBEDROG (330 315)

Description: This ¾ mile sandy beach backed by dunes and sheltered by the high headland to the south is deservedly popular.

Facilities:	Licensed café on beach with nearby toilets. Small boats can be launched over the beach. A tractor is available for hire from the car park also beach huts.
Directions:	3½ miles south of Pwllheli on the A499. Branch off left by the petrol station signposted to the Traeth.
Parking:	Pay car park on the left at the top of the beach access road.
Dogs:	Accepted.

15. PWLLHELI (375 343)

Description:	This beach stretches for three miles almost to Llanbedrog so is never crowded. Mainly fine shingle backed by dunes with ½ mile promenade. South facing though a little exposed due to wide expanse but the dunes give shelter.
Facilities:	All available in the town ½ mile inland and café & toilets at either end of the prom. Boats can be launched from slipways in the boatyards on the harbour side of the east end. A large marina in the harbour. Lifeboat.
Directions:	Pwllheli is centrally situated on the south side of the peninsula approached by the A499 from Caernarfon and A497 from Porthmadog. ½ mile causeway links the town with the promenade.
Parking:	Free along the promenade.
Dogs:	Not permitted on beach in front of promenade where they must be on a lead.

16. ABER-ERCH (399 360)

Description:	Another 3 mile long curved beach backed by dunes consisting mainly of sand and pebbles. Never crowded. Faces south.

Facilities: None near the beach but Pwllheli not far away.

Directions: Either at the far side of the harbour in Pwllheli opposite the marina. Alternatively 2 miles out of Pwllheli on the A497 Porthmadog road turn right down minor road to Aberech station and caravan park.

Parking: Free parking opposite the marina in Pwllheli. Alternatively free parking at Aberech station.

Dogs: Not allowed on a short section opposite the marina and a section fronting Aberech caravan park.

17. CRICIETH (500 380)

Description: Two beaches separated by the castle. The small west beach mainly shingle backed by promenade. The main east beach shingle and sand backed by promenade to start with then shingle bank further east.

Facilities: Toilets and cafes on both beaches. All facilities in town ¼ mile inland. Launching slipway below castle on east beach. Inshore lifeboat.

Directions: On the A497; 8½ miles from Pwllheli and 4½ from Porthmadog.

Parking: Limited free parking on west promenade; pay & display on east prom.

Dogs: Not permitted on beaches in front of either promenade.

18. MORFA BYCHAN – BLACK ROCK SANDS (530 370)

Description: A vast tract of sand stretching for 2 miles backed by dunes. Tide goes out a long way hence shallow water and a wide expanse of sand above high water. Since parking is allowed on the beach it can get crowded especially round access points. Have had trouble with water bikes and council endeavouring to regulate their use. Probably too shallow for launching all but small boats.

Facilities: Toilets behind dunes at either end. Shops ¼ mile inland.

Directions: From Porthmadog turn up by Woolworths in the main street. Follow this road for 3 miles to beach access point.

Parking: Pay on beach.

Dogs: Not allowed from the access road for a distance of 1 mile eastwards.

19. BORTH-Y-GEST (565 374)

Description: The beach at this attractive little bay on the Glaslyn estuary is not very satisfactory, but a short walk round the south headland reveals several small sandy coves with rock outcrops. Since this is an estuary, albeit a wide one, there are strong currents and care should be taken if swimming.

Facilities: Café, shop, toilets & phone by car park. Slipway for small boats.

Directions: Turn up by Woolworths in Porthmadog main street. In just under ½ mile at top of the hill fork left down to the promenade.

Parking: Free at far end of prom. Continue on foot round headland.

Dogs: No restriction.

AN INTRODUCTORY TOUR OF THE LLŶN PENINSULA BY CAR.

This day trip round the peninsula will give those unfamiliar with the area some idea of its potential and perhaps lead them to follow some of the walks described herein. It is a circular route and thus can be joined at any point, but having to start somewhere, Caernarfon as the principal town and historic capital of Gwynedd, has been chosen. Some of the roads are very narrow and winding and require care. The total distance is 112 miles and should take 5 or 6 hours excluding stops.

Assuming arrival in the area from the direction of Bangor and the A55 Expressway the motorist will find two roundabouts by the Safeway supermarket at the entrance to the town. At the second roundabout take the third exit which leads into the centre. Rounding the square note the statue of Lloyd George, WW1 Prime Minister who represented Caernarfon for over 50 years from 1890. Turn left down the hill alongside the massive walls of Edward I's castle. The Slate Quay, as its name implies, was where the product, brought down from the huge quarries inland at Nantlle, was loaded onto vessels bound for industrial England, Europe and America. Now it is a large car park and the vessels in harbour mainly pleasure craft.

Turn left before entering the car park following the road which passes the present terminus of the newly restored Welsh Highland Railway. This narrow gauge track will ultimately be restored, through Snowdonia, to Porthmadog, but at present runs for 3 miles. Continuing to a roundabout turn right and, at the bottom of the hill, turn right and immediately right again, signposted to the golf club and Coed Helen holiday park. This winding road brings you out across the harbour from the castle and is the best place to appreciate its grandeur.

The road now runs along the foreshore of Afon Menai with views across to Anglesey and the entrance to the Straits. The entrance is guarded by Fort Belan, built by the first Lord

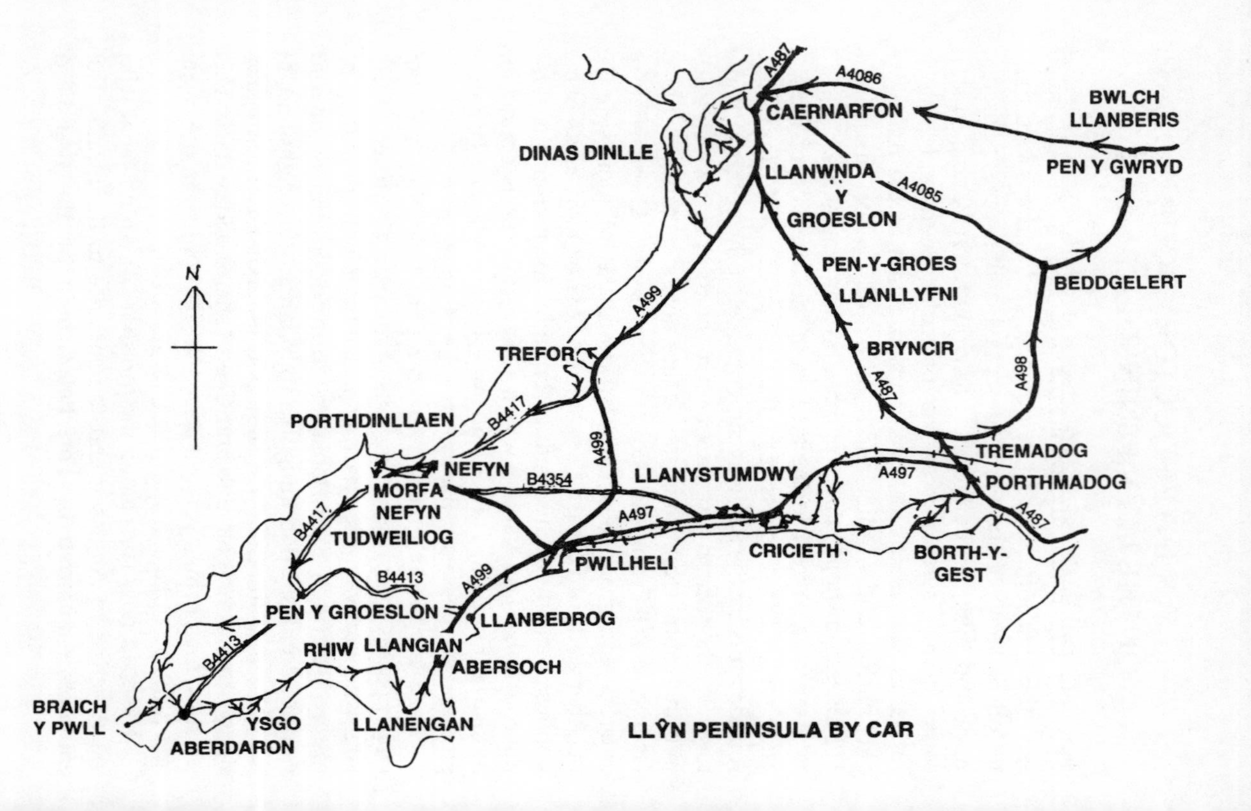
A487
A4086
BWLCH LLANBERIS
CAERNARFON
DINAS DINLLE
PEN Y GWRYD
LLANWNDA
A4085
Y GROESLON
PEN-Y-GROES
BEDDGELERT
LLANLLYFNI
A499
N
TREFOR
BRYNCIR
A498
A487
PORTHDINLLAEN
B4417
A499
TREMADOG
NEFYN
LLANYSTUMDWY
A497
PORTHMADOG
B4354
MORFA NEFYN
A497
A487
B4417
TUDWEILIOG
CRICIETH
BORTH-Y-GEST
PWLLHELI
B4413
A499
PEN Y GROESLON
LLANBEDROG
LLANGIAN
B4413
RHIW
ABERSOCH
BRAICH Y PWLL
YSGO
LLANENGAN
ABERDARON
LLŶN PENINSULA BY CAR

Newborough, at his own expense, to guard against the French at the end of the 18th.C.

3 miles after leaving the harbour, just passed a picnic site, the road turns sharply inland and just under a mile turn right at the T-junction. ½ mile further on, after the houses take the minor road on the right which runs down to Foryd Bay, popular with bird watchers, and follows round to rejoin the the wider road. Turn right and continue for the next 1½ miles to the estate village of Llandwrog, turning right in the centre. Turn right at the next T-junction and continue to Dinas Dinlle. This long beach is guarded at one end by an Iron Age hill fort and at the other, by a WW 2 airfield. There are cafes, toilets etc. here. Drive to the end of the seafront and back.

Return now along the road, ignoring the turn off to Llandwrog and continue to the main A499 road. The high wall in front surrounds the Glynllifon estate, former home of the Newborough family but now a college and country park. Turn right down this long straight road passing first through the hamlet of Pontllyfni (beware speed limit), then Aberdesach to arrive in Clynnog Fawr. The large church here, sometimes known as the cathedral of Llŷn, was an important stopping place for pilgrims en route to Ynys Enlli.

Continue a further 3 miles and turn right signposted to Trefor. In the centre of this purpose built village, dominated by the massive quarry that is its raisin d'etre, and which produced granite setts which paved the streets of industrial England, go straight ahead down a narrower street (don't follow the road round to the left) and shortly, by the de-restriction sign and a small triangle of grass with a seat, go up the narrow steep road with a sign to Cwm Pottery. 2 miles along this narrow winding road with spectacular views back up the coast, come out onto the B4417 at Llanaelhaearn.

Turning right the road runs along the southern flank of Tre'r Ceiri, on top of which is what is considered to be the finest example of an Iron Age settlement. The next village is Llithfaen, the highest in Llŷn, and further along the road there are views of the twin bays of Porth Nefyn and Porthdinllaen before dropping down to the little town of Nefyn with its long maritime association.

Turn right in the centre keeping on the B4417 but in just over a mile fork right at the diagonal X-roads in Morfa Nefyn. Turn right at the X-roads by the Linksway hotel and drop down to the beach for a fine view of Porthdinllaen with its cluster of cottages and pub on the beach. It was once considered as an alternative to Holyhead as the ferry terminal for Ireland. Return up the beach road, straight ahead at the X-roads by the hotel to shortly rejoin the B4417 and turn right.

Passing through the villages of Edern and Tudweiliog continue for 8½ miles to the X-roads at Penygroeslon. (A glance at the map shows a minor road from Tudweiliog running just inland from the coast. If time permits a visit to the lovely beaches of Tywyn and Penllech along this road is rewarding but if not the main road gives the better views of the area).

Turning right, now on the B4413 fork right in 500 yards signposted to Porthor (*Whistling Sands*). Continue for 2½ miles following the road left round the farm buildings at Methlem, signed to Aberdaron and Uwchmynydd. The entrance to Porthor is ¾ mile further on but just passed the wood in front there is a quiet picnic spot up to the right by Carreg Plas farm, from where you can get fine views of the coastline by going through the kissing gate in front and walking a little way across the field.

Carry on along the road turning right in ¼ mile at the T-junction in Carmel. Follow this narrow winding road for 1¾ mile to staggered X-roads and turn right signposted Uwchmynydd. Follow this road for 2 miles to cross a cattle grid into open heathland now at the very end of the peninsula. Follow the concrete road up to the look out at the top of Mynydd Mawr for stunning views across to Ynys Enlli (*Bardsey Island*) where it is reputed that 20,000 saints are buried, and northwards across Bae Caernarfon (Caernarfon Bay) to

Anglesey and southwards across Bae Ceredigion (Cardigan Bay) to St. David's Head in southern Wales.

Retrace the 2½ miles to the staggered X-roads and turn right to drop down to the pretty little village of Aberdaron nestling on the beach, crossing the narrow hump-backed bridge to the Ship hotel. The village has a close association with the pilgrims being the last sizeable settlement before the dangerous crossing to the island. Now a popular holiday village with a mile long beach.

Passing between the two hotels climb the steep hill out of the village passed the 12th.C. church. 2 miles out of the village take the road on the right at the X-roads by phone box on the left. Follow this narrow road round to the now deserted farm of Ysgo. For those who would like to stretch their legs see Car Walk 7.1. which details a short walk down to this tiny beach. Some consider that King Arthur fought his last battle near here at Cadlan. A little further along the road a tiny church and then another path down to Porth Ysgo. Manganese was mined in this now tranquil setting up until the 1940's. Follow the road round to the left to come back onto the road from Aberdaron and turn right to Rhiw in a mile.

Straight on through the hamlet and the spectacular 4 mile beach of Porth Neigwl (*Hell's Mouth*) opens up in front. Many a sailing ship has been wrecked here, hence its name. At the bottom of the hill is the N.T. 17th.C. manor house of Plas-yn-Rhiw. The road turns inland here and in 2 miles, after crossing a causeway keep right and then take the next right signposted to Llangian, a pretty village with interesting stone pillar in the churchyard. Passing through the village follow the signs for Llanengan village with its fine 15th.C. church. Lead was once mined in this area. The road to the right leads to Hell's Mouth car park but turn left and follow the road into Abersoch, a popular sailing centre with two beaches totalling 3 miles of sand.

Turn left by the Riverside hotel onto the A499 to Pwllheli. (Keep straight on for shops etc.). 2 miles further on come to

Llanbedrog, another holiday village with a good beach.

Pwllheli is the capital of Llŷn, once a thriving port and shipbuilding town, it now follows more leisurely pursuits, there being a new marina and sailing club which has made it the premier sailing centre for this part of the Irish Sea. Entering the town take the first street on the right just before the pedestrian crossing which leads out to the promenade, built in Victorian times on a sand bar. Turn left along the prom. and then left again at the end to run down the harbour back to the town. Turn right just before the station to follow the north side of the harbour with the marina to the right and, at the end turn left over the level crossing onto the A497 road.

Turn right and in 3 miles pass Hafan y Môr holiday camp, known to many ex-sailors, including the Duke of Edinburgh, as H.M.S. Glendower and to countless holidaymakers as 'Butlins'. In 3 miles turn left off the main road into the village of Llanystumdwy, the lifetime home of Lloyd George who lies buried here on the banks of the Afon Dwyfor. There is a museum. Rejoining the main road on the approach to Cricieth, a genteel holiday resort, turn right just passed the speed limit sign, over a narrow bridge that leads down to the west promenade. The castle, built by Llywelyn the Great in the 13th.C. separates the two promenades, and when the road drops down to the east bay turn left by the lifeboat house up into the town centre with its attractive green.

Turn right on the main road and at the top of the hill out of town there is a lay-by on the right which gives a good view back towards the castle and across the bay to Cader Idris and Harlech. Continue along the main road for 3 miles and when the road passes under a railway bridge turn immediately right into a narrow tree lined road. (Take care as the bend under the bridge hides the traffic and turn off). 2 miles along this very pretty narrow road the vast expanse of Black Rock Sands comes into view. Turning left at the bottom of the hill access by car to the beach is a short distance on the right. Continue along the road through the straggling village of Morfa Bychan with its golf club and caravan parks for 2 miles and then take the road on the right down to Borth-y-Gest. This attractive little village with a semi-circular promenade once built sailing ships but is now a peaceful holiday resort with with fine views across the Glaslyn estuary to the Rhinog range of mountains.

Turning round in the car park at the far end return back up to the main road. Turn right and drop down to the town of Porthmadog, built in the early 19th.C. by Wm. Madocks M.P. when he also built the mile long embankment across the estuary to reclaim several thousand acres of land. This and the building of the Ffestiniog railway in 1836 made Porthmadog a major port for the export of slate which lasted until after the turn of the century. The railway is now a tourist attraction and the harbour full of pleasure craft.

Turn right in the main street for the harbour and railway and left to return to Caernarfon. Go straight across the roundabout at the end of main street and a mile out of town come to the attractive village of Tremadog again built by Maddocks and the birth place of Lawrence of Arabia. Turn left in the square down Dublin street, (a reminder of the plan to make Porthdinllaen the ferry terminal), which becomes the A487, a well made road ending, after 19 miles back in Caernarfon, having passed through Bryncir, a cattle market village; Llanllyfni , Pen-y-groes and Y Groeslon former quarrying villages; Bontnewydd a dormitory village.

This ends our quick tour of the peninsula.

For those who by now are not tired of motoring and would like to see a little of Snowdonia whilst in the area an attractive alternative route back to Caernarfon which will add 10 miles and perhaps ½ hour to the round trip is as follows.

Turn right in Tremadog and follow the A498 road up through the beautiful Pass of Aberglaslyn to Beddgelert. Over the bridge in the village turn right to continue along the A498 up the Gwynant valley. Towards the top of this narrow road there is a viewpoint from where Snowdon can clearly be seen.

At the top of the hill turn left by the Penygwryd hotel where Sir Edmund Hilary and his party stayed whilst training for their successful attempt on Everest in 1953.

This road climbs up to Bwlch Llanberis (*Llanberis pass*) from the top of which the popular paths up Snowdon start. Dropping down to Llanberis village the rocks on the right are popular with climbers. Llanberis itself is the start of the Snowdon Mountain Railway and other attractions include a slate quarry museum based on the vast Dinorwig quarries that dominate the village; and, buried deep in the heart of the mountain, Europe's largest electricity pumped storage scheme.

Continuing on along the main road Caernarfon is reached in a further six miles.

Other Books About Llŷn

TOMOS O ENLLI/TOMOS THE ISLANDMAN
Jennie Jones/translated into English by Gwen Robson.
An old man's story of his life on Enlli *(Bardsey)* with wonderful woodcuts by Kim Atkinson.
ISBN 0-86381-565-0; **£4**

THIS VALLEY WAS OURS
– Eileen M. Webb. History of Nant Gwrtheyrn as remembered by one of the village's children.
ISBN: 0-86381-428-X; **£7.50**

LLŶN – THE PENINSULA'S STORY
Michael Senior; 48pp full of illustrations.
ISBN: 0-86381-443-3; **£1.95**

THE LLŶN PENINSULA MINES
– Wil Williams. A history of manganese mining on the peninsula; 64 pages; bilingual; illustrations.
ISBN: 0-86381-315-1; **£3**

Other Books About Llŷn

THE HERRING FISHERS OF WALES
– Mike Smylie. Retelling the history of the herring fisheries along the coast of Wales; 128pp;
ISBN: 0-86381-467-0; **£3.75**

ALL THE DAYS WERE GLORIOUS
Gwyn Neale. George Gissing in North Wales – quotes from Gissing's letters and diary;
ISBN: 0-86381-286-4; **£2.95**

WALKS ON THE LLŶN PENINSULA
PART 1 - SOUTH & WEST – N. Burras & J. Stiff.
ISBN: 0-86381-343-7; **£4.50**
This series combines walks with history, stories and legends. Pastoral walks as well as coastal & mountain panoramas.

WALKS ON THE LLŶN PENINSULA
PART 2 - NORTH & EAST – N. Burras & J. Stiff.
ISBN: 0-86381-365-8; **£4.50**

WALKS IN WALES – latest titles

Walks from Llandudno
CHRISTOPHER DRAPER
ISBN: 0-86381-559-6; £4.95

Circular Walks in Meirionnydd
DOROTHY HAMILTON
ISBN: 0-86381-545-6; £4.50

Walks in and around the Berwyn Mountains
JOHN TRANTER
ISBN: 0-86381-547-2; £4.50

Circular Walks in North Eastern Wales
JIM GRINDLE
ISBN: 0-86381-550-2; £4.50

The North Wales Path and 10 selected walks
DAVE SALTER & DAVE WORRALL
ISBN: 0-86381-546-4; £4.50

Circular Walks in the Black Mountains
NICK JENKINS
ISBN: 0-86381-558-8; £4.50

Walks in the Wye Valley
RICHARD SALE
ISBN: 0-86381-555-3; £4.50